COMPARATIVE LITERARY STUDIES

COMPARATIVE LITERARY STUDIES

An introduction

S. S. Prawer

Taylor Professor of German
in the University of Oxford

BARNES & NOBLE
BOOKS
10 East 53d St., New York 10022
(a division of Harper & Row Publishers, Inc.)

Published In The U.S.A. 1973 by
HARPER & ROW PUBLISHERS, INC.
BARNES & NOBLE IMPORT DIVISION

© 1973 S.S. Prawer

ISBN 06 495698 9

Typesetting by Specialised Offset Services
Limited, Liverpool
Printed in Great Britain by
Redwood Press Limited, Trowbridge, Wiltshire

Contents

FOR DAVID
עליו השלום

Preface

This book has five efficient causes. First, the fate I shared with millions of others: of having been raised within one cultural and literary environment and then, in impressionable years, finding myself suddenly cast into another, whose differences from and likenesses to the first have never ceased to preoccupy me. Second, the fact that German literature — the first love to which, *quand même*, I am always driven to return — has proved throughout its history unusually hospitable to the literature of other countries, assimilating it through translations and adaptations, and allowing it to stimulate native productions which show its influence and yet are uniquely German. Third, the conviction, gained as a university teacher in Great Britain, Germany and the U.S.A., that studies of a foreign culture can best be pursued by those who have a firm basis in their own and that, conversely, 'What shall they know of England/That only England know?' applies as fully in the literary field as it does in geography, sociology and politics. Fourth, the gratitude I feel, not only to the poets, novelists and dramatists of many nations, cultures and climes, whose work has so greatly enriched my life, but also to the critics whose knowledge and understanding of more than one literature has helped me to chart my way. Chief among these is H. Stefan Schultz, with whom I was privileged to work, for a year, in the University of Chicago; a man of wide reading in many languages, deep learning, literary sensitivity and humane concern, for whom Comparative Literature is not so much a discipline with its own circumscribed subject-matter as a daily practice, almost as natural and as necessary as breathing. To the delight and profit of his students and colleagues, Professor Schultz

constantly illuminated particular texts of Schiller, Goethe,
Hölderlin, Stefan George or Hofmannsthal by drawing,
pertinently and tellingly, on the Greek, Latin, English and
French classics. The names of other scholars crowd in upon
me: René Wellek, Roy Pascal, Leonard Forster, Wolfgang
Clemen, Harry Levin, Ulrich Weisstein, René Etiemble,
Ronald Peacock, R.A. Sayce, Albert Béguin, John Bayley,
Peter Demetz, Dámaso Alonso, Claudio Guillén, Robert
Auty . . .; they bring in their wake the memory, sometimes of
personal contacts, always of books and essays that have shed
light in dark places, and helped me to see the particularity of
works in one language through comparison and contrast with
works in another. Their arguments and examples will appear
often in the following pages; it would be too much, however, to
hope that they would all have approved of the context in which
I have placed them.

Fifth and last: my desire is to do something to counter an
all-too-prevalent notion that comparative literary studies are
irremediably extrinsic and unspecific; that Comparative
Literature encumbers scholars with 'devices of factitious
synthesis and the distraction of pointless cross-reference'.
The words just quoted are those of Damian Grant, who has
put the case against Comparative Literature (as he sees it)
with vigour and succinctness.

The comparatist is content to ignore the varied contour of imaginative
achievement (which can only be discovered at ground level, by footing
it over the hills) as he hovers purposeless above the unrelieved tract of
literature, making readings that decrease in value as he gains in
altitude [. . .] The whole approach encourages a talking *round*
literature rather than providing a first-hand impression of imaginative
intuitions realized in language [. . .] A point, in geometry, has position
but no size; one sometimes feels that the individual work approaches
the same condition in the sated gaze of the literary historian, and the
jigsaw mind of the comparatist.[1]

Against this view the present book tries to set a descriptive
typology of comparative literary study which shows its
significant work on the detail as well as the overall contours
of the literary map. It describes the different kinds of

[1] *Times Literary Supplement*, 19 March 1964, p. 235.

investigation carried out by scholars and critics who have brought together, habitually or occasionally, works written in different languages, giving brief examples from their work or supplying illustrations of my own. I have not tried to write a history of the subject or to mention all the main works, even in English — hence the absence of such important landmarks as Edmund Wilson's *Axel's Castle* and the books of C.M. Bowra, Mario Praz and Frank Kermode. My examples are taken, in the main, from the literatures with which I am myself best acquainted: British, American, German and French; but I hope that, supplemented by side-glances at others, these will serve their purpose of making a general point which is of interest even to those who have ranged much further afield.

I am grateful to my colleagues R.A. Sayce and E.L. Jones for reading the first draft of the book and suggesting improvements; also to J.L.I. Fennell, C.F. Robinson and J.M. Thomas, who patiently answered my questions and corrected some at least of my misapprehensions.

I am also grateful to the following for permission to use copyright material: the Clarendon Press, Oxford, for the poem by Czeslaw Milosz from *Polish and Hungarian Poetry 1945-56,* ed. George Gomöri, 1966; Alfred A. Knopf, Inc., and Martin Secker and Warburg Ltd., for excerpts from *Journals 1889-1949* by André Gide, trans. and ed. Justin O'Brien, Harmondsworth 1967; and Verlag Helmut Küpper vormals Georg Bondi, Düsseldorf und München, for Stefan George's translation of a poem by Verlaine (*Stefan George: Werke,* Ausgabe in zwei Bänden, 1958).

1.
What is Comparative Literature?

It has long been recognized that the term 'comparative literature', current in England since its casual use by Matthew Arnold in the 1840s,[1] is not altogether happy. Apparently analogous terms from the natural sciences are not open to the same objections: 'comparative anatomy' makes sense, for anatomy is a mode as well as an object of study, while 'literature' is nowadays an object only. One must stress this 'nowadays'; for as René Wellek, who has gone into the history of this and related terms most thoroughly, recently demonstrated, the word 'literature' has in fact narrowed its meaning.[2] 'An Italian of considerable literature' signified, to Boswell, a man of learning and literary culture; this meaning survived into the nineteenth century, but is now obsolete. 'Literature' now means (besides 'the body of books and articles that treat of a particular subject') 'literary productions as a whole', 'the writings of a country or period, or of the world in general'. The term 'comparative literature' therefore lays itself open to such charges as have been brought against it by Lane Cooper in the 1920s: a 'bogus term' he called it, one that makes 'neither sense nor syntax'. 'You might as well permit yourself to say "comparative potatoes" or "comparative husks".'[3] I therefore prefer, like

---

[1] 'How plain it is now, though an attention to the comparative literatures for the last fifty years might have instructed any one of it, that England is in a certain sense *far behind* the continent' (letter to his sister, May 1848). It will be noted that Arnold here still speaks of 'the comparative literatures' rather than 'comparative literature', and that — like Madame de Staël before him — he looks to other literatures for touch-stones by which to try the writers of his own country.

[2] René Wellek, *Discriminations: Further Concepts of Criticism*, New Haven 1970, p. 1 ff.

[3] Wellek, op. cit., p. 4.

Lane Cooper, the clumsier but more accurate description 'the comparative study of literature', though I will occasionally, for the sake of brevity, use the more established term. German and Dutch have avoided this difficulty through the use of a present participle and a noun-compound: *vergleichende Literaturwissenschaft* describes our activity more precisely than the adjectival formation used in English, and more satisfactorily too than the past participle used in the French *littérature comparée*.[4]

'Comparative literature' implies a study of literature which uses comparison as its main instrument. But, as Benedetto Croce never tired of pointing out in his vigorous attack on the notion that *letteratura comparata* could form a separate discipline, this is true of any study of literature: we cannot fully appreciate the individuality of Wordsworth, his place in a tradition and modification of that tradition, without comparing his work, explicitly or implicitly, with that of Milton and James Thomson, that of Shelley and Keats. Comparative literature, then, makes its comparisons *across national frontiers*. But here again we come up against a difficulty. If we compare the greatest German novel of development and education, Goethe's *Wilhelm Meister's Apprenticeship* [*Wilhelm Meisters Lehrjahre*], with *Indian Summer* [*Der Nachsommer*], a novel in the same tradition by the Austrian writer Adalbert Stifter, and that with another such novel, *Green Henry* [*Der grüne Heinrich*], written by the Swiss Gottfried Keller — are we then making a contribution to comparative literary studies? In one way we undoubtedly are, for the national traditions of Germany, Austria and Switzerland, and the different political and social ambience of those countries, may help to account for important differences of tone, style and subject-matter. Stifter and Keller, however, for all their close attachment to their native region, rightly regarded themselves as writers within the great

[4] The difference between the German and French terms might, in fact, form the basis of an exercise in comparative stylistics. It illustrates a tendency in modern French, noted by Albert Malblanc, to use static terms where German uses dynamic ones: *sûr* as against *treffsicher* [=accurate of aim] and *zielbewusst* [=sure of one's goal], *fatal* as against *unheilbringend* [=bringing illfortune, pernicious], *étrier* as against *Steigbügel* [=stirrup], *la mer est grosse* as against *die See geht hoch* [=the sea is high, the sea is rough]. Albert Malblanc, *Stylistique comparée du francais et de l'allemand,* Paris 1961.

tradition of German literature; assessment of the differences between them is the province of the Germanist. Comparative literary studies as they are generally understood, and as I understand them in this book, operate, then, across *linguistic* barriers. In that sense it would seem legitimate to treat as the object of such study the work of a man who writes competently in more than one language: Yvan Goll, for instance, who used French and German with almost equal facility, Samuel Beckett, at home in English and French, and Vladimir Nabokov, whose early work is in Russian and whose later work is in English. To do justice to the achievement of these men a critic has to be polyglot in a wider sense than a critic who attempts to do justice to the work of an Anglo-Irish poet like Yeats or Anglo-American poets like Eliot and Pound.

A distinction is often made between what is called 'Comparative' and what is called 'General' Literature. R.A. Sayce has furnished a succinct statement of the differences between the two: 'General Literature' he defines as 'the study of literature without regard to linguistic frontiers', 'Comparative Literature' as 'the study of national literatures in relation to each other'.[5] This is a useful distinction so long as we recognize that the concept of 'national' literature is not without its problems, and that the two kinds of study must, inevitably, shade into one another. When we trace the development of the Sonnet in Europe since Petrarch's day we are contributing to 'General Literature' — as we always do when we discuss questions of literary theory, poetics, and principles of criticism in a supra-national context. But when, in the course of such a survey, we compare a Shakespearean sonnet with a Petrarchan one, we are within the area of 'Comparative Literature'. That these two activities are ultimately inseparable should need no further demonstration.

We have now begun to do what modern Linguistics, from which most humanistic disciplines have something to learn, has taught us: to look at our key-terms not in isolation but in associative and lexical fields.[6] The lexical field of 'Comparative Literature' includes, besides the term

[5] *Yearbook of Comparative and General Literature* XV (1966), p. 63.

[6] cf. Wellek, op. cit., p. 13.

4   *Comparative Literary Studies*

'General Literature', that of 'World Literature' or *Welt-literatur*. This term, hallowed by its use in the later work of Goethe, has acquired many disparate meanings, of which three are important in our context. The first of these is implied by its occurrence in the title of many a history of literature: it describes the attempt to write such a history on a global (or at least a European) basis, by juxtaposing chapters and sections on the various national literatures, or by describing various movements, currents or periods in as many countries as possible. The possibilities and dangers of this kind of historiography have been notably analysed by J. Brandt Corstius.[7] Secondly, 'World Literature' has been used to signify 'great books', 'classics', 'the best that has been written in the world': the *Odyssey*, the *Oresteia*, the *Aeneid*, the *Divine Comedy, Faust, Madame Bovary, The Magic Mountain* may all be said to belong in this category. More important than either of these, however, is the third use of the term, which we owe to Goethe: he meant by *Weltliteratur* awareness of national traditions other than your own, openness to works written in other countries and other languages, traffic and exchange between the various litera-tures which would parallel and supplement commercial traffic and exchanges.[8] This does not, of course, imply the abandonment of national traditions or the disappearance of national literatures. André Gide, in fact, when he commented in a diary entry for 9 October 1916 on the need to 'Europeanize' culture, came very close to Goethe's view of the matter. In the middle of a world war Gide felt the need to immerse himself in a culture born out of 'the various literatures of our old world, each of them powerfully

[7] J. Brandt Corstius, 'Writing histories of world literature', *Yearbook of Comparative and General Literature* XII (1963), pp. 5-14.

[8] cf. Fritz Strich, *Goethe und die Weltliteratur*, Berne 1946, pp. 13-27. Goethe's parallel between material and cultural exchange is characteristically elaborated in the *Manifesto of the Communist Party* composed by Marx and Engels in 1848: 'The bourgeoisie has through its exploitation of the world market given a cosmopolitan character to production and consumption in every country.... In place of the old local and national seclusion and self-sufficiency, we have intercourse in every direction, universal interdependence of nations. And as in material, so also in intellectual production. The intellectual creations of individual nations become common property. National one-sidedness and narrow-mindedness become more and more impossible, and from the numerous national and local literatures there arises a world literature [*Weltliteratur*]' (Karl Marx, *Selected Works*, London 1942, vol. I, p. 209).

individualized'. And only, he added, in a passage which would have won Goethe's assent, 'the particularization of literature, only its nationalization, could permit the Europeanization of culture'.[9] The great difference is that Goethe increasingly looked beyond Europe; that in his later years he tried to come to terms with the literature and culture of the East (Persia, the Arab countries, India) as well as that of his native continent. The very titles of his later poetry-cycles — *West-östlicher Divan, Chinesisch-deutsche Jahres- und Tageszeiten*[10] — speak of the effort he made to fructify German literature through contact with remoter literatures and cultures.

Weltliteratur, in Goethe's sense, is clearly related to Comparative Literature and may lead comparatists to ask many of their most interesting questions. How is the 'canon' of great authors formed? Why are Lucan and Statius given such importance in Dante's *Divine Comedy*? Why was it Virgil rather than Homer who seemed the great model to epic poets before the seventeenth century?[11] Why had Dostoevsky come to appear more and more important in twentieth-century Europe?[12] Why did General de Gaulle, when asked to name the three greatest figures in European literature, answer: 'Dante, Goethe and Chateaubriand'? How eccentric is de Gaulle's assessment and how representative?[13] A search for the answer to many such questions must lead into social and political as well as cultural territory. One need not be a profound sociologist, however, to appreciate the difference

[9] André Gide, *Journals 1889-1949*, translated, collected and edited by Justin O'Brien, Harmondsworth 1967, pp. 257-8.

[10] 'Divan' means 'assembly' or 'group': Persian poets used this word to describe a collection of poems. 'West-Eastern Collection'; 'Chinese-German Seasons and Times of Day'.

[11] cf. Ulrich Weisstein, *Einführung in die vergleichende Literaturwissenschaft*, Stuttgart 1968, p. 109.

[12] cf. Lionel Trilling, 'The fate of pleasure: Wordsworth to Dostoevsky', in *Romanticism Reconsidered: Selected Papers from the English Institute*, ed. Northrop Frye, New York 1963, pp. 73-106.

[13] Quoted by George Steiner in 'The Uncommon Market', *The Times* (Saturday Review), 14 August 1971. Steiner adds. that when asked 'And what of Shakespeare?' de Gaulle replied: 'You said *European* literature'. 'In de Gaulle's preferences,' Steiner comments, 'we can observe a unitary aesthetics, a set of criteria about the gravity and decorum of high intellectual, poetic forms' characteristic of French classical sensibility and schooling.

between René Etiemble's plea, in his stimulating *Comparaison n'est pas raison* of 1963, that we should follow Goethe's example by looking beyond Europe for our canons of excellence and for a challenge to new literary effort, and the attitude of the well-meaning Frenchman who taught Léopold Senghor during his student days at Dakar:

The Reverend Director of the Collège Libermann, at Dakar, never stopped repeating to us: that our ancestors had not created a civilisation. They had left us only a *tabula rasa* on which everything had yet to be inscribed. When, in our youthful spirit of opposition, we asked for linen garments he replied by sending us back to our accustomed loin-cloths. And he added, as a clinching argument, that we allowed ourselves to be charmed by the music of words instead of clinging to their substance: their meaning. That, of course, was decisive proof of our lack of civilisation.[14]

---

[14]   Léopold Sédor Senghor: *Ansprachen anlässlich der Verleihung des Friedenspreises des deutschen Buchhandels*, Frankfurt 1968, pp. 44-8. English readers may here recall Lord Macaulay's famous blast against supporting the study of Arabic and Indian literature and culture among Queen Victoria's Indian subjects: 'I am quite ready to take the Oriental learning at the valuation of the Orientalists themselves. I have never found one among them who could deny that a single shelf of a good European library was worth the whole native literature of India and Arabia [...] I have certainly never met with any Orientalist who ventured to maintain that the Arabic and Sanscrit poetry could be compared to that of the great European nations. But when we pass from works of imagination to works in which facts are recorded, the superiority of the Europeans becomes absolutely immeasurable. It is, I believe, no exaggeration to say, that all the historical information which has been collected from all the books written in the Sanscrit language is less valuable than what may be found in the most paltry abridgment used at preparatory schools in England. In every branch of physical or moral philosophy, the relative position of the two nations is nearly the same [...] It is said that the Sanscrit and Arabic are the languages in which the sacred books of a hundred millions of people are written, and that they are, on that account, entitled to peculiar encouragement. Assuredly it is the duty of the British Government in India to be not only tolerant, but neutral on all religious questions. But to encourage the study of a literature admitted to be of small intrinsic value, only because that literature inculcates the most serious errors on the most important subjects, is a course hardly reconcilable with reason, with morality, or even with that neutrality which ought, as we all agree, to be sacredly preserved. It is confessed that a language is barren of useful knowledge. We are to teach it because it is fruitful of monstrous superstitions. We are to teach false History, false Astronomy, false Medicine, because we find them in company with a false religion [...] I would at once stop the printing of Arabic and Sanscrit books, I would abolish the Madrassa and the Sanscrit college at Calcutta' (Minute addressed by Macaulay to Lord Bentinck, Governor General of India, on 2 February 1835). In the same Minute, Macaulay stated clearly what should be the ultimate aim of education in India: 'We must at present do our best to form a class who may be interpreters between us and the millions whom we govern; a class of persons, Indian in blood and colour, but English in taste, in opinions, in morals, and in intellect. To that class we may leave it to refine the vernacular dialects of the country, to enrich those dialects with terms of science borrowed from the Western nomenclature, and to render them by degrees fit vehicles for conveying knowledge to the great mass of the population.'

It is not the least important task of those who further comparative literary studies today to extend their scope, and their terms of reference, sufficiently to break down what remains of such benevolent cultural imperialism: a task made easier by the fact that Milman Parry, Albert B. Lord and C.M. Bowra have accustomed us to widening our sense of 'literature' sufficiently to include oral material.

No one reader, obviously, can keep in his mind a personal canon that includes the whole of world literature. Each must make his own selection, find his own path, discover what authors, what works, have the deepest affinity with his own nature. Many will still be inclined to assent to the characteristic injunction given by Sainte-Beuve when he came to discuss, in the *Causerie du lundi* of 24 October 1850, the question 'What is a Classic?':

'My Father's house has many mansions' — let this be true of the Kingdom of the Beautiful no less than of the Kingdom of Heaven. Homer, as always and everywhere, would be the first in such a realm, the most resembling a god; but behind him, like the procession of the Magi, would stand those three magnificent poets, those three Homers so long unknown to us, who composed immense revered epics for the ancient nations of Asia: Valmiki and Vyasa the Hindus, and Firdusi the Persian. In the domain of taste it is a good thing to know at least that such men have existed, so that the human race is seen as a whole. *Having paid our respects, however, we should not linger in these distant climes.*[15] (author's italics)

There are readers and writers, however — one thinks of Hermann Hesse, for instance, or of Arthur Waley — who feel a profound shock of recognition in the face of non-European literature and thought; for whom the fusion of East and West is a necessity; whose personal canon must include Li Tai Po and Confucius as well as Goethe and Keats. These may then become mediators between European readers and extra-European writers and help to widen the choice available

---

[15] The translation I have used is that by Francis Steegmuller and Norbert Guterman in their *Sainte-Beuve: Selected Essays*, London 1963, p. 8. Harry Levin, in a recent lecture, echoed Sainte-Beuve's sentiments: 'What shall it profit our students to gain Swahili and have no Latin?'

to Western readers in search of a literature of personal affinity.[16]

In the chapter of his *Discriminations* to which I have already had occasion to refer, René Wellek lists other terms that enter into the field of meaning of which 'Comparative Literature' forms part: terms like 'learning', 'letters', and *belles lettres* (competing for a place with 'literature'); terms like 'universal literature' and 'international literature' (competing with 'comparative literature' or *Weltliteratur*). Enough has now been said, however, to permit a working definition of 'comparative literary study' as conceived in this book:

An examination of literary texts (including works of literary theory and criticism) in more than one language, through an investigation of contrast, analogy, provenance or influence; or a study of literary relations and communications between two or more groups that speak different languages.

In two important ways, this differs from the definition of Claude Pichois and A.M. Rousseau[17] which in other respects it resembles. First it breaks with the notion that one cannot be a comparatist unless one deals with more than one national culture: a notion which will be found more of a hindrance than a help when discussing the work of bilingual authors like Beckett or multilingual regions like Alsace and Switzerland. By this I do not, of course, mean to deny or belittle the role that national and regional traditions have always played in the genesis and development of literatures. Many would now reject conceptions of national character based on biological differences; but no one in his senses can refuse to recognize divergences due to the social, educational, geographical and historical forces that have shaped the different nations and their writers. Nor does my definition include, secondly, any reference to that wider function which

---

[16] cf. Ronald Peacock's valuable distinction between two functions of literature: 'On the one hand we can distinguish a public and social function, in the sense that literature enshrines a vast total of thought, feeling, and experience gathered through the centuries since literary creation began and which is available in a certain measure, partially rather than completely, to everyone; and on the other hand, an individual, personal, function, because it can be selectively treated by individuals and assimilated to the process of their own thought, sensibility and spiritual character.' (*Criticism and Personal Taste*, Oxford 1972, p. 14).

Henry H. Remak tried to induce comparative literary studies to perform: 'the studies of relationships between literature on the one hand and the other areas of knowledge and belief, such as the arts, philosophy, history, the social sciences, the sciences, religion etc., on the other hand.'[18] Investigation of such other 'areas of knowledge and belief' is indeed important for the illumination of literary facts — but it has no place in a definition which sets out to distinguish the province of the 'comparatist' from that of other literary scholars.

Not that even then the province can be marked out absolutely. How does one define 'different languages'? There are those who see modern British and American English, or German and Swiss-German, as different linguistic systems, while others try to distinguish between *diglossic* and *bilingual* situations. When an inhabitant of Zürich switches to High German he shows his diglossic competence, but when he switches to excellent French he shows that he is bilingual.[19] One may recognize relative diversification: Graham Greene's English and Salinger's American are less diversified than (say) German and Dutch, or Spanish and Portuguese. And one may well recall Max Weinreich's wry epigram, out of a life-time spent in the effort to have Yiddish recognized as a language in its own right: 'A language is a dialect that has an army and a navy.'[20] This is a border-area, and there will always be times when dispute is possible.

It is also important to point out that the term 'literature', in our context, need not invariably refer to the best and highest that has been written — to works that have entered, or are ever likely to enter, the canon of a nation's literary

[17] *La Littérature comparée*, 2nd ed., Paris 1967, pp. 174-6.

[18] Remak's much-discussed definition of Comparative Literature as 'the comparison of one literature with another or others, and the comparison of literature with other spheres of human expression', first appeared in *Comparative Literature: Method and Perspective*, ed. N.P. Stallknecht and H. Frenz, Carbondale 1961, p. 3.

[19] These questions are fully discussed in Uriel Weinreich's *Languages in Contact*, 2nd ed., The Hague 1963, and Leonard Forster's *The Poet's Tongues: Multilingualism in Literature*, Cambridge 1970.

[20] cf. John Lyons, *New Horizons in Linguistics*, Harmondsworth 1970, p. 19: 'In origin at least a standard language is simply a dialect which, for historical and linguistically "accidental" reasons, has acquired political and cultural importance in a particular community.'

classics. Like other scholars, comparatists will often be well advised to look beyond the classics, to examine more humble writings of entertainment and instruction. The work of Balzac, Dickens and Dostoevsky, for instance, as Donald Fanger and others have pointed out, can be significantly illuminated by a study of the Gothic novel, the boulevard novel, the penny-dreadful, the *roman-feuilleton*, melodrama and the police gazette. Like Shakespeare before them, the great nineteenth-century novelists were able to take over the elements of popular entertainments and make them reveal potentialities unsuspected before.

Accounts of the history of comparative literature studies often resolve themselves into a history of the terms *'Littérature comparée'* and 'Comparative Literature' — which goes back no further than the early nineteenth century, when the French term came into use in emulation of Cuvier's *Anatomie comparée*; or into a history of the subject as an academic discipline, which begins sporadically with a series of courses by Noël and Laplace at the Sorbonne (*Cours de littérature comparée*, 1816-1825) and gathers momentum about the middle of the nineteenth century. But, in fact, literatures from various cultures and in various languages had been 'compared' ever since the time when the Romans measured their own poetry and oratory against that of the Greeks; and reference to works in several languages came naturally to the leaders of taste who proposed a catholic view of Western literature in the Renaissance.[21] When Latin lost

---

[21] Those who investigate Renaissance and pre-Renaissance literatures in any European language cannot do justice to their theme without becoming comparatists. What Keith Whinnom has said of 'distortions' in Spanish studies applies no less beyond the borders of Spain: 'The first form of distortion with which I want to deal arises from the fact that people devote themselves to the study of "Spanish" literature at all. They are blinkered, from the outset, by this concept "Spanish". The resultant distortion is a good deal less important for modern literature, where linguistic barriers, though permeable, do tend to wall off the literatures of Europe one from another, but for Renaissance literature, and even more for medieval literature, it is momentous [...] It would be an inaccurate generalization to affirm that all the substantial works of Spanish medieval literature are translations. But an extraordinarily high proportion of the major works are freely adapted translations, amplified glosses, amalgams of borrowed passages and *topoi*, and close imitations of medieval Latin (and in some cases medieval French or Arabic) works [...] If we fail to take medieval Latin literature into account, Spanish medieval literature becomes a series of miracles.' (*Spanish Literary Historiography: Three Forms of Distortion*, Exeter 1967, pp. 6-9.) Peter Ganz's study of 'Tristan, Isolde und Ovid' (*Mediaevalia Litteraria*, de Boor Festschrift, Munich 1971, pp. 397-412) may serve to demonstrate how much light may be shed on medieval texts in the vernacular by a comparison with classical (as well as medieval) Latin literature.

its position as a 'universal' language, and growing nationalisms divided Europe more and more, comparative literary studies assumed new functions: that of restoring a lost unity and universality, or that of enriching narrow native traditions by beneficial contacts with others. Increasingly, too, comparatists looked beyond the Western world: to the Indian classics at first, with the German Romantics; to Arab, Persian and even Chinese literature, with Goethe; and in our own time to other far Eastern as well as to African literary and oral traditions. As new and subtler methods of analysis and classification benefited literary studies of all kinds, comparisons across linguistic frontiers were used to shape (by contrast) a sense of native traditions, to alter (by example) the course of a particular national literature and to construct (with unrestricted width of reference) a general theory of literature.

The work of August Wilhelm Schlegel illustrates the first of these, that of Matthew Arnold the second, and that of Friedrich Schlegel the third. And increasingly, as Sainte-Beuve observed in the *Revue des deux mondes* (September 1868), comparative literary studies were pursued in a spirit of 'purely intellectual curiosity' which set them apart from the overtly interested polemics of Lessing or Voltaire. They have since then often been in danger of sinking in the swamps of positivism, of degenerating into a collection of facts not related to any first-hand experience of literature, or of becoming the kind of thing described, with justifiable dislike, by Damian Grant (see above, p. x); but as often they have been saved by gifted scholar-critics, inside the universities as well as outside them, and by poets, dramatists and novelists who have not only responded to works written in other languages but also recorded their response in critical essays. Such men have usually seen Comparative Literature as

an object rather than a subject — an objective Anglicists and Americanists will share when they view their respective fields in the fullest orientation.[22]

They have tended to believe, with Anthony Thorlby, that

---

[22] Harry Levin, *Countercurrents in the Study of English*, Vancouver 1966, p. 29.

Comparative Literature does not in itself commit one to any other principle than that comparison is a most useful technique for analysing works of art, and that instead of confining comparisons to writings in the same language, one may usefully choose points of comparison in other languages [...] To see one poem, or one picture, or one building is to have little feeling for its qualities. To see another example of the 'same' thing, which being another work of art is of course not the same but only 'comparable', is to take the first step towards recognising what is in each case good, original, difficult, intended.[23]

They have tried, with Lilian Furst, to achieve through comparative studies

a more balanced view, a truer perspective than is possible from the isolated analysis of a single national literature, however rich in itself.[24]

Behind their work, as often as not, lies the conviction first stated by Friedrich Schlegel in his celebrated essay 'On the Study of Greek Literature' (1795-6):

Torn from their context, and looked at as separate entities existing by themselves, the different national portions of modern literature are inexplicable. Only in relation to each other can their tonality and definition[25] be properly assessed. But the more carefully one regards the whole body of modern literature, the more that too appears a mere part of a larger whole.[26]

They are as convinced as Matthew Arnold that

everywhere there is connection, everywhere there is illustration: no single event, no single literature, is adequately comprehended except in relation to other events, to other literatures.[27]

What follows is an attempt to illustrate how such maxims may work out in critical practice.

[23] 'Comparative Literature', *Times Literary Supplement*, 25 July 1968, and *Yearbook of Comparative and General Literature* XVIII (1968), pp. 78-9.

[24] *Romanticism in Perspective: A Comparative Study of Aspects of the Romantic Movement in England, France and Germany*, London 1969, p. 277.

[25] The precise significance of the term *Haltung*, which Schlegel uses here, is disputed. The rendering 'definition' follows a suggestion by Professor Hans Eichner.

[26] Friedrich Schlegel, *Sämmtliche Werke*, Vienna 1823, vol. V, pp. 40-41.

[27] Matthew Arnold, *On the Modern Element in Literature*. Inaugural Lecture delivered in the University of Oxford, 14 November 1857.

2.
National Character and National Literature

The most ambitious type of comparative literary study is that which undertakes to define and compare different national traditions: the 'spirit' of French literature, say, with that of German or English literature. Generalizations based on such dubious entities usually bear out Max Weber's observation in *The Protestant Ethic and the Spirit of Capitalism*: 'The appeal to national character is generally a confession of ignorance'. It was Weber himself, however, who demonstrated the possibility of constructing 'ideal types': groups of characteristics which may never be found together in any one individual case, but which yet constitute a true type, a meaningful, unified analytical entity. In comparative literary studies, such 'ideal types' have frequently been constructed especially since Mme de Staël's attempt, in her book on German literature and society, *De l'Allemagne*,[1] to distinguish between the German and the French man of letters at the turn of the century. Heine's polemical counterblast to Mme de Staël, also called *De l'Allemagne* in its French version, probed deeper into social, political and intellectual motivation, but did not materially alter the 'ideal types' of the socially-orientated French and the solitarily brooding German writer which his predecessor had constructed with admirable verve, much over-simplification and no small measure of truth.[2] That such constructs deteriorate easily, in the hands of lesser men, into stereotypes that hinder international understanding instead of furthering it, their history amply demonstrates.

[1] Mme de Staël, *De l'Allemagne*, London 1810.

[2] In his meticulously documented and level-headed study *Germany in the Eighteenth Century: The Social Background of the Literary Revival* (Cambridge 1935), W.H. Bruford found himself able to confirm, and pay grateful tribute to, Mme de Staël's distinctions.

Valuable observations can be made by literary men who have come to appreciate, through many detailed stylistic studies, what particular effects different languages allow writers who work within them. Such observations occur frequently, for instance, in Dámaso Alonso's book on Spanish poetry, *Poesia Española*.[3] Through constant comparison of Spanish poems with poems in other languages, Alonso details effects that are possible in Spanish but not in French poetry, because word-order may be varied much more radically in Spanish than in French. While true of Spanish, this observation applies even more strongly to the Latin poetry of ancient Rome as compared with that in any modern European language. It is much more difficult, on the other hand, to obtain in Spanish the stark rhythmic effects possible in English (effects such as those achieved by Gerard Manley Hopkins in his experiments with 'sprung rhythm') because Spanish has fewer monosyllabic words, and fewer words with masculine endings. In this respect, Alonso maintains, Italian versification has an advantage over Spanish because of the greater possibilities of apocope — the very opening line of the *Divine Comedy* exhibits this characteristic by its shortening of *cammino* to *cammin*: 'Nel mezzo del cammin de nostra vita'.[4]

Related to such observations are attempts made by Theodore Savory and others to describe the sound-systems characteristic of different languages. In classical Greek, for instance, Savory finds a harmoniousness and musicality which he attributes, in large measure, to the abundance and variety of vowels and diphthongs and the relative inconspicuousness — except when special effects demand them — of harsh consonants and consonantal clusters:

Greek words that end in consonants almost always end in γ or ρ or ς, and very seldom in any other. The lightness which this alone imparts to a Greek sentence is sustained and amplified by the frequency of the brighter vowels α, ε, and ο, and the rarity of the hard, anaemic ι and υ.[5]

---

[3] Dámaso Alonso, *Poesia Española*, Madrid, 1957.

[4] 'Midway in our life's journey.'

One need not agree that ι and υ are rightly described as either 'hard' or 'anaemic' to concede Savory's general point — particularly when he goes on to insist that sound should not be considered apart from the syntactic and semantic features of a given language. The passage on Greek vowels and consonants is therefore followed by remarks on characteristic patterns of stress and accentuation and on the precision and elegance of utterance made possible by the Greek particles and by the Greek system of declensions and conjugations.

Savory's descriptions of the Greek, English and French languages[5] may be regarded as a first step in the direction indicated by George Watson, who has said that the most challenging prospect for the future of Comparative Literature is the definition of what one literary language will allow and what another will not. He has called for an examination, on a comparative basis, of the *sound* that characterizes a given language, and the unique way a poem may exploit that sound; adding the riders that in specific instances sound must always be related to sense, and that such researches might well be supplemented by studies of the metres which characterize the great literary languages.[6]

Recent interest in narrative perspective has brought closer scrutiny of the way different languages allow combination and shifting of narrative tenses. A great deal of attention has been paid, for instance, to what is known as *style indirect libre, erlebte Rede* or 'free indirect discourse' — a type of narrative internal monologue or discourse not introduced by verbs of saying or feeling. What would have been the first person in direct speech:

'Do I really have to go to the dance?'

becomes third person in *style indirect libre*:

Did she really have to go to the dance?

In French and German, as in our English example, a shift of tense is mandatory when the narrative containing the passage in free indirect discourse uses the epic preterite. What would have been present tense in direct speech (*'Do* I really have to ... ?) becomes 'past' tense (*'Did* she really have to ... ?).

---

[5] Theodore Savory, *The Art of Translation*, new and enlarged edition, London, 1968, pp. 61f., 82f. and 92f.

[6] George Watson, *The Study of Literature*, London 1969, p. 112ff.

In Russian, from the time of Pushkin onwards, the tense that would have been appropriate in direct speech can be retained in *style indirect libre*: the 'heavy thought' that stirs the mind of Pushkin's *Prisoner in the Caucasus* (1822) therefore opens in the present tense, to change to the past as the prisoner's mind turns to the past: 'A distant path *leads* to Russia, to the land where he *began* his youth without cares . . .' (my italics). This possibility has been explored in English too; by a subtle Australian writer, for instance, who here renders a young man's thoughts about his grandfather's death:

Well, his grandfather *is* dead. An old man, whom he loved, but at a at a distance, amongst woodshavings. (my italics).[7]

In German, moreover,

there is another type of indirect discourse without governing intro-duction (verba dicendi/sentiendi etc.). This type is characterized by the subjunctive corresponding to the tenses of direct discourse and by two forms of reproducing questions: one corresponding to the word order of direct discourse, the other corresponding to the word order and the use of the conjunction 'ob' (in questions of decision) in ordinary indirect discourse. Usually this type is restricted to the reproduction of speech.[8]

The different degrees of immediacy and remoteness, of irony and identification, that may be obtained by authors making use of these differing possibilities in the various languages, remain to be evaluated.

Comparisons between the type of effect possible in one language and those possible in another have frequently been made by men who have tried to render the classics of Greece and Rome accessible to fellow-countrymen unable to read Greek and Latin. Translators from the Latin never cease to complain that when they try to reproduce the sense and rhythm of a Latin sentence they are forced to use many more words than can be found in the original. Latin, they sigh, has no articles, definite or indefinite; it can condense a subject

---

[7] Patrick White, *The Tree of Man*, Toronto 1955, London 1956 (Harmondsworth 1961, p. 478).

[8] Günter Steinberg, *Erlebte Rede: Ihre Eigenart und Formen in neuerer deutscher, französischer und englischer Erzählliteratur*, Göppingen 1971, II, pp. 360 and 376.

and its predicate into a single word; it is far less cluttered by pronouns and prepositions than most modern languages. Latin, it has therefore been said, has a harder, more 'brazen' sound than English; one can hear, in Roman literature, 'the sound of a great nation'.[9] This is a tentative connexion one may legitimately make; but it is all too easy to pass from this to the kind of exaggeration in which Willa Muir indulged when she spoke of her valuable pioneer work as a translator of Kafka:

I find myself disliking the purposive control, the will to power dominating the German sentence. I dislike its subordination of everything to these hammerblow verbs; I dislike its weight and its clotted abstractions. I have the feeling that the shape of the German language affects the thought of those who use it and disposes them to overvalue authoritative statement, will power, and purposive drive. In its emphasis on subordination and control it is not so ruthless as Latin, but both in Latin and in German the structure of the language, I am inclined to think, conditions the kind of thought that it expresses. And so it must have an organic relation to the aspirations and imaginative constructions of those who use it. A language which emphasizes control and rigid subordination must tend to shape what we call *Macht-Menschen*. The drive, the straight purposive drive, of Latin, for instance, is remarkably like the straight purposive drive of the Roman roads. One might hazard a guess that from the use of *ut* with the subjunctive one could deduce the Roman Empire. Could one then deduce Hitler's Reich from the less ruthless shape of the German sentence? I think one could, and I think that is why I have come to dislike it.[10]

It would take a good deal of hindsight to 'deduce' Hitler's Reich from the shape of the German sentence, though one could perhaps make out a case for saying that the German language, with its many possibilities of co- and sub-ordination, its boxing of clause within clause, and its multivalent words (*Geist, aufheben . . .*) is particularly well adapted to certain kinds of speculative philosophy. André Gide, reading Kleist in the middle of the Second World War, confided to his journal a more generous assessment of the linguistic resources of German.

[9] Rolfe Humphries, 'Latin and English verse — some practical considerations', in *On Translation*, ed. R.A. Brower, Galaxy edition, New York 1966, p. 57.

[10] Willa Muir, in *On Translation*, ed. Brower, ed. cit, p. 96.

I am reading the *Penthesilea* very slowly, letting nothing pass without understanding and feeling it completely, with indescribable rapture. Kleist makes wonderful use of German syntax, and this makes it possible to appreciate its resources, its subtle licence, its suppleness. The fine tangle of the sentence, in which he frolics, remains almost impossible in French, where the function of uninflected words is most often indicated only by their position. Enough to form two very different nations.[11]

The last sentence of this passage may help us to see the kernel of truth in Willa Muir's pardonable exaggerations. There is some truth, after all, in the notion that the limits of our language indicate the limits of our world.

Historically, attempts to define the 'spirit' of different nations as reflected in their language and literature are of great importance: for some of the most striking advances made in our understanding of cultural evolution were made by men like Herder and A.W. Schlegel who attempted synoptic views and enormous syntheses based on wide reading of literary and other texts in many languages. They were also deeply aware of the historical dimensions of literary scholarship, and would have agreed with the view that comparisons of national traditions and characteristics are meaningless unless they are confined to something less amorphous than the notion of an over-all and unchanging 'national character', and to something more specific than the total characteristics of a nation's literature — though here again it is possible, on occasions, to take a bird's eye view and compare (say) the continuously evolving traditions of English and French literature with the more 'discontinuous' traditions of Germany. For the most part, however, comparisons will be most fruitful when they confine themselves to a given historical period and a given, historically evolving genre. Roy Pascal, for instance, in the concluding chapter of his work on *The German Novel*,[12] suggested that in the best German novels the struggle between personal and social values tends to take the form of a struggle between the claims of inner, transcendental values and outer social reality; that

[11] Gide, *Journals, 1889-1949*, ed. cit., p. 695 — 13 October 1942.

[12] Roy Pascal, *The German Novel*, Manchester 1956.

the *Bildungsroman*, the novel of education and development, is peculiarly German in that it deals essentially only with the weaning of the heroes from their inwardness, with their spiritual preparation for social life, and stops or falters when they actually enter upon it; that the best German novels tend to lack 'plot', variety of incident, and that their symbolism tends to be prominent and heavy. By contrast:

The English novel is rich in symbolical situations which fully belong to the actual world of the story and have a natural function in the narrative, and at the same time sum up the inward, moral situation. All the elements of a story are in fact in this sense symbolical, but certain of them stand out startlingly, revealing the very heart of the matter. One thinks of Robinson Crusoe discovering the footprint, Maggie Tulliver drifting with Stephen down the Floss, the excursion to the Marabar caves in *A Passage to India*; in these typical examples the occurrence seems to 'exist for itself' at the same time as it brings into evidence a whole moral crisis. In the German tradition the symbol is more forced, it often seems to come from another world.[13]

But the German novelists, Pascal goes on to show, recognized earlier than the English the limits of realism and story-telling, and evolved modes of seeing the world, and shaping it imaginatively, towards which other European novelists have only groped in our own day. Through his comparison of the German, English and French literary traditions, Pascal is able to make his readers more sharply aware of the limitations and virtues of each; to show not only 'that there is no German *Madame Bovary*, *Le Rouge et le noir*, or *Anna Karenina*' but also that there is no English *Nachsommer* or *Doktor Faustus*. As J.P. Stern puts it in a book that largely confirms Pascal's findings:

From Goethe's *Werther* (1774) and *The Elective Affinities* (1809) through Rilke's *Notebooks of Malte Laurids Brigge* (1910) to Thomas Mann's *Doktor Faustus* (1947) the twin themes of solitude and isolation have formed a major aspect of German prose; hence my claim that in the exploration of solitary experience lies its major contribution to world literature.[14]

---

[13] op. cit., p. 304.

[14] J.P. Stern, *Idylls and Realities: Studies in Nineteenth Century German Literature*, London 1971, p. 179.

Inductive generalizations of this kind are useful ordering schemes within which exceptions and individual differences can be discussed. They must not, of course, become critical myths; it would be wrong, for instance, to allow the magnificent German achievements in the sphere of the *Bildungsroman* to blind us to the many other forms and modes which German novelists employed even before the days of Fontane and Raabe.[15]

Constructions like those of Pascal and Stern, attempts to 'place' whole segments of national literatures in relation to the literatures of other nations, can be helpful in discussions of individual writers. In his little book on Saul Bellow, Tony Tanner has attempted to show Bellow's awareness of *Welt-literatur* and to relate his work to European as well as American traditions. Tanner notes the tributes Bellow has paid to Russian writers, particularly Tolstoy and Dostoevsky; and while remaining fully aware of the differences between these (fundamental differences suggested by the very copula in George Steiner's *Tolstoy or Dostoevsky*), Tanner nevertheless seeks to sum up what Bellow could hope to gain from the traditions of the nineteenth-century Russian novel.

The great Russian writers often assert, with irresistible conviction, the ability of the human spirit to deny and invalidate a whole range of false social values and reaffirm the priceless freedom, independence, and integrity of the self. Most importantly, it was the Russian writers who most vividly questioned and opposed the nineteenth century ideals of materialistic pleasure and comfort as the means of human progress. Contemporary American society has often provoked Bellow into making similar indictments. Many of his characters, too, refuse society's values and dislodge themselves from its drift in order to celebrate the independence and freedom of the self alive. But Bellow's important characters do not stay underground, and Dostoevsky's profound and lacerating metaphysical ironies are replaced by something more euphoric and affirmative.[16]

This is well said, and provokes three reflections. First, that Tanner discerns the effect of reading the great Russian novelists as being for the most part a matter of diffused

[15] An admirable account of these will be found in Friedrich Sengle's *Biedermeierzeit. Deutsche Literatur im Spannungsfeld zwischen Restauration und Revolution, 1915-1848*, vol. II (*Die Formenwelt*), Stuttgart 1972.

[16] Tony Tanner, *Saul Bellow*, Edinburgh 1965, pp. 7-9.

atmosphere and moral attitude rather than of specific variations on Russian themes. Second, that while he does not go into the difference of quality between a novel by Dostoevsky and one by Bellow, one could easily conceive of a comparison which uses Dostoevsky as a standard against which to measure Bellow, a comparison which would show up the relative lack of resonance and creative power in the American writer. Third and most important: Tanner's generalization about the spirit of Russian literature is a reflection of Bellow's own — he is seeing the nineteenth-century Russian novelists through the eyes of an American writer of the twentieth century, just as other critics have tried to see them through the eyes of Thomas Mann and Hesse, Gide and Camus. We are thus passing from direct to mediated generalizations; from speculations about the nature of a specific country's achievements in a given period of literature to studies of the *image* or *mirage* of a country's literature in the minds of another nation's writers.

Such studies can take many forms. One may ask questions like these: What did Goethe know of English literature? What generalizations did he make about it? Which authors attracted him most? What discernible effect did his reading of English authors have on his work at various stages of his life? What relation has Goethe's image to the image (or images) in our own minds, today?[17] From here it is only a step to the kind of study represented by Simon Jeune's book on American types in French literature.[18] This kind of study, the study of the image, not of national literature, but of national types, in the writings of another country, has been formidably attacked by René Wellek. In 'The Crisis of Comparative Literature'[19] and elsewhere, Wellek has accused the champions of such studies of 'dissolving literary scholarship into social psychology and cultural history', and denied their right to the status of literary critics. My own feeling is that literary scholarship need not be quite so purist — sociological and historical investigations have a legitimate

[17] cf. James Boyd, *Goethe's Knowledge of English Literature*, Oxford 1932.

[18] Simon Jeune, *De F.T. Graindorge à A.O. Barnabooth — Les types américains dans le roman et le théâtre français 1861-1917*, Paris 1963.

[19] René Wellek, *Concepts of Criticism*, New Haven 1963, pp. 284-8.

part to play in comparative literary studies, and comparatists perform a useful function when (for instance) they expose misconceptions about national characteristics and national types propagated by widely read novelists. Such an exposure has been notably attempted by Arturo Barea in an essay on Hemingway's *For Whom the Bell Tolls*.[20] Barea details various errors in the social ordering of Hemingway's Spanish characters, in their psychology and motivation, and — above all — in their speech, and concludes:

> Reading *For Whom the Bell Tolls*, you will indeed come to understand some aspects of Spanish character and life, but you will misunderstand more, and more important ones at that.
>
> Ernest Hemingway does know 'his Spain'. But it is precisely his intimate knowledge of this narrow section of Spain which has blinded him to a wider and deeper understanding, and made it difficult for him to 'write the war we have been fighting'. Some of his Spanish conversations are perfect, but others, often of great significance for the structure of the book, are totally un-Spanish. He commits a series of grave linguistic-psychological mistakes. He has understood the emotions which 'our people as a whole' felt in the bull-ring, but not those which it felt in the collective action of war and revolution.

By analysing minutely the misconceptions that lie behind such utterances as Agustin's 'Also I have a boredom in these mountains' (when, in reality, a Castilian peasant would not use the abstract word *aburrimento* [=boredom] but would say something like *Además me aburro·en estas montañas* or *Estas montañas me aburren*), Barea is able to demonstrate the spuriousness of Hemingway's realism and relate this to his failure to render adequately the complex feelings and sensations of men engaged in a specific civil war. His study tells us something about Hemingway's art while illuminating, at the same time, Barea's own intentions and achievement in *The Forge, The Track* and *The Clash*.

The question of generalizations about national character is raised in one of the seminal works of aesthetics, Lessing's *Laocoon*. The starting-point of this treatise is a comparison made by J.J. Winckelmann between the Laocoon figure in Virgil and that which appears in a piece of late Greek

[20] Arturo Barea, 'Not Spain but Hemingway', in *The Literary Reputation of Hemingway in Europe*, ed. R. Asselineau, New York 1965, pp. 198-210.

statuary. Virgil's Laocoon screams when attacked by a sea-serpent: 'clamores horrendos ad sidera tollit';[21] the statue shows him with his mouth only slightly opened, groaning rather than crying aloud. In an early work, Winckelmann had referred this difference to one of national character: the Greeks kept their anguish in, sought to preserve their ideal of noble simplicity and tranquil grandeur even in the midst of terrible affliction and passion; the Romans knew no such restraint. Lessing demolishes this argument easily enough, citing instances from Homer and the Greek tragic poets in which heroes appear screaming with pain; he refers the difference Winckelmann had rightly noted, not to a difference in national character, but to one in artistic medium. If your ideal is visual beauty, a gaping hole in the middle of the face is clearly not consonant with it. Lessing thus conveys a salutary warning (and one that has not lost its point even today) against premature conclusions about 'national character'; against conclusions arrived at without consideration of the limitations imposed on artists by the medium in which they work, or of the conventions and ideals which circumscribed work in that medium at a given time.[22] The point has its importance in many areas of literary investigation which do not involve comparisons between the different arts — in genre-study, for instance.

One aspect of this search for exemplifications, in literature, of different national attitudes and traditions has produced some particularly interesting work recently: examination of the way in which different works of fiction, written at different times and in different languages, depict historical events. This is the subject of one of the classics of Marxist criticism, George Lukács's *The Historical Novel*, which lays due emphasis on the work of Sir Walter Scott. In the course of an analysis of Balzac's possible debt to Scott, D.R. Haggis has followed up Lukács's hints and has tried to specify what it was a writer could learn from the Waverley novels. *Les Chouans*, he maintains, is a milestone in Balzac's career 'not simply because Balzac had learnt from Scott's talent for description and incidental detail,

---

[21] 'His shrieks were horrible and filled the sky' — *Aeneid* II, W.F. Jackson Knight's translation, Harmondsworth 1958, pp. 57-8.

[22] cf. Peter Demetz, 'Die Folgenlosigkeit Lessings', *Merkur* XXV (1971), p. 731.

or from the way Scott had presented the representatives of a
primitive race, or even because he had suggested to Balzac ways
in which his novel might benefit from a visit to the scene of its
action and from listening to first-hand recollections of past
times, but because *the reading of Scott had shown how the
writing of fiction might be related to political and historical
reflection and analysis'* (my italics).[23] John Bayley, however,
has recently attempted to revise one aspect of Lukács's work.
In his discussion of Pushkin's *The Captain's Daughter* Bayley
charges Lukács with failing to distinguish sufficiently clearly
between Scott's spirit and outlook and those of Pushkin. In the
England of Scott and his successors, the past did not invade the
present: it could be comfortably distanced in the way
suggested by the subtitle of Waverley: *'Tis Sixty Years Since.*
'The typical literary use of the past in post-Napoleonic Europe
was as an escape from the present.' Pushkin's Russia, in this
respect, resembled not contemporary England, but the
England of Shakespeare:

A growing national self-awareness, founded on recent victories and the
emergence of the nation on the European scene; a vogue for the
national past, as introducing — and exemplifying — a present full of
insecurity; problems of succession, threatened rebellion, an oppressed
and often mutinous peasantry; a censorship.

While Pushkin takes Scott as a model for plot and situation,
he remains aware of the relevance of the past to the present
in a more immediate way than Scott; the disputed succession
in *Boris Godunov* is as relevant to Pushkin's Russia as that in
Richard II was to Shakespeare's England at the time of the
Essex rebellion. Bayley therefore discerns much less historical
romanticism in Pushkin than in Scott, and drives his point
home by contrasting the depiction of a rebellion in *Old
Mortality* with that in *The Captain's Daughter*:

When it comes to the rebellion itself, Scott's genius turns against him. It
is not that he evades the grim side of it, but as a good North Briton he
is concerned to present the '45 as the very stuff of antiquity [. . .]

---

[23] D.R. Haggis, 'Scott, Balzac, and the historical novel as social and political
analysis: *Waverley* and *Les Chouans'*, *The Modern Language Review* 68 (1973), p.
68.

Waverley's love for Flora MacIvor and admiration for the Young Pretender are generous and misguided day-dreams which he will recall with the nostalgia of maturity remembering the follies of youth. Grinev's experiences and acquaintance with Pugachev are by contrast premonitory, deeply educative, haunting not in their recall of the past but by revealing the scope and shadow of the future.

Scott's art puts history behind us. Pushkin, in *The Captain's Daughter* no less than in *The Bronze Horseman* and *Poltava*, brings it into the present and leaves it to imply what is to come.[24]

The parallel between Scott and minor Russian novelists like Zagoskin may be close; for Pushkin's historical romances the closest parallel is provided by Shakespeare's history-plays. In this as in many other respects Pushkin shows himself as a great interpreter of the historical situation of Russia after Peter the Great. What Bayley has done, while building on foundations laid by Lukács, is something particularly important in all comparative literary study: he has deepened our sense of the difference between Scott and Pushkin, their individuality and their rootedness in a particular historical situation, in the very process of analysing the way in which the work of one was 'dependent' on that of the other.

Pushkin is a writer who invites the comparative approach almost more than any other. Few authors have so consciously made themselves an intermediary between their own time and country and the literatures of other times and climes. From the critical observations scattered throughout his writings, both public and private, one could compile — it has been said — a quite detailed history of European literature. In the face of every literary achievement he seems to have asked himself: could that be done in Russian? Where others were content to read, assimilate, think over and criticise, he tried to 'repeat the process of creation'.[25] That, surely, is what lies behind Dostoevsky's famous tribute: 'Pushkin alone, among all the world's poets, possesses the faculty of completely reincarnating in himself an alien nationality.'[26] Yet here we must heed Pushkin's own hint, in the projected Preface to

---

[24] John Bayley, *Pushkin: A Comparative Commentary*, Cambridge 1971, pp. 109, 349-50.

[25] cf. V. Setschkareff, *Geschichte der russischen Literatur*, Stuttgart 1962, pp. 78-9.

[26] Dostoevsky, *The Diary of a Writer*, translated by B. Brasol, New York 1954.

Boris Godunov, that the idea of writing the play came to him after the study of Shakespeare, Karamzin and ancient Russian chronicles. It is precisely his faculty of combining, in the alembic of his own talent, material from foreign and native sources, which makes him so important a figure in the history of European literary relations.

Studies of 'relation' and 'reception' used to loom larger in comparative literary research than they do now; they have left behind some impressive monuments which may well inspire younger scholars to continue along the same lines, despite all the objections that have been raised against them as 'extrinsic', and as therefore irrelevant to any genuine appreciation of individual literary works. There are two-way studies of great scope, like Brian Downs's continuing investigations of Anglo-Scandinavian literary relations, all published in *The Modern Language Review*; more limited two way studies, like C.L. Waterhouse's,[27] or Eudo C. Mason's book on the German and English Romantics;[28] comprehensive one-way studies, like Philippe Van Tieghem's study of foreign influences on French literature[29] and Horst Oppel's examination of literary relations between England and Germany;[30] more limited one-way studies like F.W. Stokoe's elegant, well researched *German Influence in the English Romantic Period*[31] and Enid Starkie's *From Gautier to Eliot*.[32] The materials and methods used in such studies do not differ in any essential way from those used in monographs on the reception of a national literature, or part of a national literature, by a given writer, and in monographs on the reception of a given writer in a country other than his own.

---

[27] C.L. Waterhouse, *The Literary Relations of England and Germany in the Seventeenth Century*, London 1941.

[28] Eudo C. Mason, *Deutsche und englische Romantik*, Göttingen 1959.

[29] Philippe Van Tieghem, *Les Influences étrangères sur la littérature française*, 2nd ed., Paris 1967.

[30] Horst Oppel, *Englisch-deutsche Literaturbeziehungen*, 2 vols., Berlin 1971.

[31] F.W. Stokoe, *German Influence in the English Romantic Period*, Cambridge 1926.

[32] Enid Starkie, *From Gautier to Eliot: The Influence of France on English Literature 1851-1939*, London 1960.

There is one particular set of questions, however, which the authors of the larger surveys must not be allowed to shirk. Which were the periods that saw especially intensive literary relations between two given countries? What were the factors — cultural, social, political, economic — which facilitated relations of this kind? What was it that the reading public, and the authors, of a given country sought and found in the foreign literature they welcomed?

A comparatively simple example would be the very rapid and extensive assimilation of American writings, particularly fiction and drama, in Germany after 1945. Among the factors which played a part in this was the cultural isolation in which Germans had lived under Hitler, cut off by government decree from many of the sources of European Modernism — post-war Germany showed itself, therefore, particularly anxious to make up for lost time. The demand for books, which resulted from this, was satisfied in part by the *Amerikahäuser* put up and generously stocked by the occupying American forces. At the same time Fulbright and other grants took hundreds of people across the Atlantic and back, while a host of visiting American professors spread the fame of Dos Passos, Faulkner, Hemingway and younger transatlantic authors. Nor must it be forgotten that Germany had a great tradition of assimilating other cultures through translation, a tradition which was now revived by gifted translators like Friedhelm Kemp and Hans Hennecke, who could count on the support of enterprising publishers. Publishing houses were encouraged (sometimes with subsidies) to bring out American authors in excellent German versions that soon found their way into the ever-growing series of paperback editions. The Hollywood film-industry also played its part: its products, usually running in German cinemas in expertly dubbed versions, brought a number of minor writers, from Margaret Mitchell at one end of the scale to Raymond Chandler and John Steinbeck at the other, to the attention of Germans, who then proved eager to read the book on which the film had been based. Many of the writers who drew a large and appreciative public and earned the acclaim of German intellectuals were not those whom Americans themselves would have placed in the first rank.

One of the most highly esteemed dramatists, for instance, was Thornton Wilder, whose *The Skin of Our Teeth*, under the title *Wir sind noch einmal davongekommen*, spoke with startling immediacy to post-war Germany, to a generation which had seen its world collapse around it. Wilder's plays also helped to bridge a gap in Germany's own severed tradition: for their techniques were inspired by those of the European avantgarde of the twenties and early thirties, the techniques of the Expressionists, in fact, whom Hitler had proscribed as degenerate and whose work was now becoming available again. Germans repaid Wilder with a critical acclaim which (even in an intelligent work like Peter Szondi's *Theorie des modernen Dramas*, 1956) must seem to English-speaking readers as excessive as English acclaim of Gautier's *Mademoiselle de Maupin* seemed to cultured Frenchmen at the end of the last century.[33]

An equally interesting case is that of Thomas Wolfe, whose works became respected and popular at about the same time as those of Wilder. As recently as 1957 Günter Blöcker felt moved to compare Wolfe to Novalis.[34] Wolfe's fiction struck Germans as one vast *Bildungsroman*, with added anarchic elements that endeared it to a generation sick of being regimented; they relished Wolfe's concern about formation of the self, his obtrusive symbolism and metaphysical aspirations. It is not surprising, therefore, to find that Blöcker singles out for praise the spirit-conversation and the dance of the marble angels at the end of *Look Homeward, Angel.* Once again, it was their own as well as the American past which Germans were here discovering; Wolfe, it may be remembered, had himself felt such affinity with German culture and artistic endeavour that in the twenties, when other American expatriates clustered around Gertrude Stein, Fitzgerald and Hemingway in Paris, he took up residence in Germany.

Once American fiction, new and old, became known in

---

[33] Veneration of Wilder is not confined to critics or to Germany: the Swiss dramatist Friedrich Dürrenmatt ended a speech accepting a doctorate at Temple University with the words: 'I close with the expression of my opinion that your Thornton Wilder is one of the greatest contemporary authors.' (*Journal of Modern Literature*, Temple University, Philadelphia, I, (1970, p. 91.)

[34] In *Die neuen Wirklichkeiten*; the comparison remains unchanged in the third edition, Berlin 1961, p. 206.

post-war Germany, it could not fail to strike its readers as familiar within its strangeness and foreignness. Many of its traditions are in fact akin to German traditions: American cultivation of the short narrative, the *nouvelle*, from Hawthorne to Henry James; the Gothic horror constituent of American literature, from Poe to Faulkner; its marriage of realistic elements with a frequently heavy symbolism, from the time of Melville to that of Wolfe and Wilder — all these were elements Germans could recognize as akin to their own literature. In addition, however, the post-war generation also found elements that seemed refreshingly unfamiliar and therapeutic: Hemingway's laconic, apparently unemotional mode seemed precisely what was needed by a people which had been subjected to an unprecedented barrage of rhetorical and demagogic appeals, a people sick of large words and exaggerated gestures.[35]

The study of literary relations need not, of course, confine itself to the interplay of just *two* countries. Harry Levin once undertook a study that looked closely at the response of Russian, French and English readers, just after the Second World War, to contemporary American literature, and showed how each country selected elements most appropriate to its own needs and problems. Russian critics fastened on writers like Theodore Dreiser and Upton Sinclair, whose formally unadventurous novels seemed to convey a realistic picture of capitalism and its discontents, while Sartre adapted, in *The Reprieve*,[36] those techniques of Dos Passos which seemed most suitable for the presentation of the theme of disorder within an ordered literary structure. British commentators, Levin concludes, sought new opportunities for satirizing Anglo-Saxon attitudes, Russian Marxists sought

[35] cf. Graham Hough's account, in *The Last Romantics* (London 1961), of the reception of French literature in England at the end of the nineteenth century: 'French literature, formally more constrained, has always been psychologically more experimental than English, and what the English writers of the eighties and nineties found in France was not so much new modes of experience as precedents for talking about them. Often enough, French writing was really revealing the English writers to themselves, making genuine aspects of their sensibility articulate for the first time. Swinburne's algolagnia would have been the same if no other literature had ever existed; but without Gautier and Baudelaire he would have had considerable difficulty in finding means to express his abnormalities' (op. cit., p. 191).

[36] *Le Sursis*, 1945.

a vindication of their party-line, French existentialists sought new means of presenting the conditions of their own existence — and in twentieth-century American literature they all found something which answered their needs.[37]

In international literary relations, the process of challenge and response therefore acts in two ways. On the one hand, the existence of a distinguished body of literature in one language acts as a challenge to readers in another to widen their experience by responding to it as fully and appropriately as possible — translators, expounders, adapters and imitators will further this task in their different ways. On the other hand, particular literary developments, never wholly independent of developments in social, economic, scientific and philosophical fields, will themselves constitute a challenge, to which the enthusiastic reception of a given body of writings — Italian in Shakespeare's England, English in the Germany of Lessing and Herder, German in the France of the Napoleonic and post-Napoleonic period — supplies an appropriate response. Appreciation of this two-way relationship of 'emitter' and 'receiver' is essential to any understanding of literary fortunes and the mediators who further them.

[37] Harry Levin, 'Some European views of American Literature', in *The American Writer and the European Tradition*, Minneapolis 1950, pp. 169-80.

3.
Reception and Communication

Besides compiling the longer studies of literary relations just examined, comparatists have frequently edited and examined the correspondence of two important authors across national and linguistic frontiers;[1] brought together and interpreted all available evidence of an author's reading in foreign literature;[2] traced the different ways in which an author embedded quotations from, and allusions to, a foreign author in his own work;[3] shown how an author took over whole chunks of a foreign work without acknowledgement (as Brecht took over, into his plays, large portions of Karl Klammer's translations from Villon and Rimbaud); traced reminiscences of foreign works (like the parallels that can be found between Dostoevsky's *The Insulted and the Injured* and Dickens's *Old Curiosity Shop*); or tried to determine what kind of impulses to original creation a writer may have received from works in a foreign language. All such studies are concerned with direct contact rather than typological analogy; but here as elsewhere, these two categories must not be too thoroughly divorced. An author's readiness to make direct contact with another's work, and to allow it to affect his own literary creations, must depend on a feeling of kinship, or fascinated hostility — feelings which also play their part in determining the reception of a given author's work in a country other than his own. Such studies of reception, diffusion and 'literary fortune' form an important part of comparative studies. In the wrong hands they degenerate, all too easily,

[1] C.E. Norton, *The Correspondence between Goethe and Carlyle*, London 1887.
[2] J. Boyd, *Goethe's Knowledge of English Literature*, Oxford 1932.
[3] S.S. Prawer, *Heine's Shakespeare: A Study in Contexts*, Oxford 1970.

into mechanical catalogues; it is therefore worthwhile to look in some detail at a small-scale work which does not degenerate in this way, but makes exemplary use of the materials that scholars engaging in this kind of exercise have first to collect and then to interpret. Such a study is Roger Asselineau's investigation of the fortunes of Ernest Hemingway's work in France.

Asselineau begins by examining the chronology of French translations of Hemingway's work during the inter-war period, together with the articles and reviews they provoked as they appeared. This indicates early French interest in these writings, followed by a lull, followed by renewed interest in 1931-2. In 1932, Asselineau goes on to note, Gallimard published a translation of *A Farewell to Arms* by M.E. Coindreau: a fortunate event for Hemingway, for he was now being published by the most influential and energetic firm in the French publishing world, appearing alongside Gide and Jacques Rivière, and his new translator was one of the most gifted practitioners of that difficult art. Coindreau later turned against Hemingway and attacked him in *Les Cahiers du Sud*; at the beginning of the Second World War interest in his work slackened, to be revived again after 1945.

To illuminate the background of Hemingway's success in France between 1928 and 1932, Asselineau then provides an analysis of French taste, and French social and cultural life, during those years. He points to the vogue of the novel-form; to the many calls for a change in the subject-matter and tone of the French novel; to the great interest shown, during this time, in the exotic and in travel-books; to a general disillusionment and 'nouveau mal du siècle'; to the exaltation, in the work of Malraux, of energy, heroism and vitality in the midst of absurdity and sadness. From this he passes to more specific factors which favoured Hemingway's success: Hemingway lived in Paris after the First World War, and was personally known to a number of French writers who spread his fame; the U.S.A. established herself as one of the great powers and Europeans were eager to know more about her; revolts against mass-production and standardization found support and confirmation in certain aspects of Hemingway's fiction; moods of despair and nihilistic revolt were detected

in Hemingway's work which seemed to parallel such moods
in contemporary France; those who were repelled by
Puritanism welcomed Hemingway's frankness about sexual
matters. Above all: Frenchmen were attracted by the energy
and vitality these fictions seemed to celebrate, by a directness
and lack of intellectuality which offered, they felt, a
refreshing contrast with French writings of the same period;
realizing at the same time that what appeared as directness
and closeness to life was the result of a subtle art of
understatement, foreshortening, omission and counterpoint.
Discerning critics were aware how much Hemingway had in
fact learnt from the European novelists of the nineteenth
century, and perceived that when French readers thought
they were discovering the U.S.A. in Hemingway's fiction,
they were, in fact, as often as not, rediscovering the
techniques of French writers transplanted to America.

Asselineau goes on from there to discuss the later
fluctuations of Hemingway's reputation and literary fortunes,
the new Byronism made up of disenchantment and tough
nihilism fostered by his work, and the fructifying influence it
had on the work of Sartre and Camus. We need not follow
him any further, except to note that his study can serve as a
model because it discriminates sensibly between the
authority and resonance of different critics, assessing anew in
each case how much weight may be given to a critical
pronouncement on an author's work; because it takes into
account, in a sensitive and well-informed manner, many
sociological factors – the different types of reader Hemingway found at different times, for instance – and political/
historical factors; and because it makes its readers aware of
the importance of the communications industry in fostering
reputations – newspapers, the cinema, advertising, the very
name and reputation of a great publishing-house all play their
part. In addition, Asselineau shows adequate understanding
of the strengths and weaknesses of Hemingway's writings as
well as the development of his art from *A Farewell to Arms*
and *The First Forty-Nine* to *For Whom the Bell Tolls* and
Across the River and into the Trees, and demonstrates
constantly his ability to distinguish between literary values
and the values of the book-trade. Asselineau's essay justly

points, throughout, to the inadequacy of purely quantitative methods. It shows, concretely and convincingly, that every piece of information must be diligently collected, but that it must also be weighed and assessed.

A more complex undertaking than Asselineau's is that represented by Friedrich Gundolf's book on Shakespeare's fortunes in Germany.[4] Without neglecting intermediaries (like the 'English Comedians' who performed adaptations of Shakespeare's plays in seventeenth-century Germany) and critical pronouncements, Gundolf devotes most of his flair and energy to analysing in detail the impact Shakespeare's work had on that of Germany's writers — on the work, particularly, of Lessing, Goethe, Schiller and the Romantics. It dicusses various translations of Shakespeare, and traces the fortunes of his favourite verse-form in German blank-verse drama from Wieland to Schiller. Gundolf's book, although burdened with a mandarin style, remains an important contribution to German literary and intellectual history. It could only have been written by a man who knew his Shakespeare thoroughly in the original; a knowledge which implies some understanding of Shakespeare's Elizabethan and Jacobean ambience. This enabled Gundolf to discuss, meaningfully, the inevitable distortions Shakespeare suffered at the hands of even so gifted a translator as August Wilhelm Schlegel, and to produce a classic of comparative criticism.

Gundolf's work is important because it shows not only the diffusion of Shakespeare's work in Germany, but also the different ways in which the development of German literature dictated the manner of its reception and the aspect of it which was assimilated at different times: how Shakespeare supplied, successively, examples of dramatic subjects (*Stoff*), modes of tragedy and comedy different from those of France (*Form*) and a spirit and approach to literature and life which went beyond either (*Gehalt*). Gundolf's analysis is paralleled, on a smaller scale, in T.S. Eliot's essay *From Poe to Valéry* (published in 1948): a sketch of the manner in which three French poets, representing three different generations,

---

[4] Friedrich Gundolf, *Shakespeare and the German Mind* (*Shakespeare und der deutsche Geist*), Berlin 1911.

responded to the work and career of an American fellow-poet, Edgar Allan Poe. Baudelaire, in Eliot's view, appreciated in Poe the prototype of a *poète maudit*, and in this sense was interested above all in Poe *the man*. He saw in him what Harry Levin was later to describe as 'the poet as orphan, alienated from his cruel step-parent society by its crass philistinism'; this view he found confirmed by Poe's *stories*, of which he produced masterly translations. With Mallarmé, in Eliot's view, interest shifts to Poe's *poetic technique*, to the author of *poems* which must seem better to men whose native language is not English than they do to English-speaking readers; while with Valéry, Eliot claims, it is neither the man nor the poetry but the *theory* which engages attention. Above all, Valéry is fascinated by Poe's essays *The Philosophy of Composition* and *The Poetic Principle*, in which the making of poetry is presented as a far more coolly calculating, intellectual exercise than in effect it seems to have been for Poe. But Eliot does not merely tell us that in Valéry we may find the culmination of ideas which can be traced back to Poe — the development of an interest in the compositional process, and in observing oneself in the very act of composition, which has reached its apogee in our own day. He shows himself concerned for the future and puts forward, at the end of his essay, a hypothesis which the history of poetry is, I believe, tending to confirm: 'that this advance of self-consciousness, the extreme awareness of and concern for language which we find in Valéry, is something which must ultimately break down, owing to an increasing strain against which the human mind and nerves will rebel.' What begins as a somewhat over-schematic piece of literary criticism (for interest in the various aspects of Poe was not, of course, as neatly divided between three poets and three generations as Eliot suggests) turns in the end into an analysis of the state of poetry today — a state for which Eliot himself can claim no small measure of responsibility — and a tentative projection of its future.

A still narrower focus than the type of reception study suggested by *From Poe to Valéry* is provided by books and essays that trace the fortunes of a single work in a given country or period — the fortunes of *Hamlet* in Germany, for instance, have been admirably sketched by Walter Muschg in an essay in his *Studies in the Tragic History of Literature*;[5] or by enquiries into the relation of a single writer to a fellow-writer in another language. A useful enquiry of this latter kind concerns the relation of Henry James to Flaubert, which can be studied in the two essays James devoted to Flaubert (1893 and 1902), in *obiter dicta* scattered through James's prefaces, essays and journals, and — of course — in the novels themselves. For a brief illustration, however, we cannot do better than glance at Ronald Peacock's discussion of T.S. Eliot's dealings with Goethe.[6]

Peacock's point of departure is a notorious passage from Eliot's *The Use of Poetry and the Use of Criticism* (1933):

Of Goethe perhaps it is truer to say that he dabbled in both philosophy and poetry and made no great success of either; his true role was that of the man of the world and sage — a La Rochefoucauld, a La Bruyère, a Vauvenargues.

Taken out of context, this statement does indeed constitute a critical blunder: its absurdity will appear at once to anyone who has sufficient German to read Goethe's poems in the original. If, however, we look at the statement in its context, if we ask how Eliot came to make it, we may see in it — besides plain ignorance of Goethe's work — the not illogical outcome of a particular aesthetic and philosophical point of view in a particular historical situation. The context which Peacock then sketches around Eliot's pronouncement includes the history of Goethe criticism in England; the change in orientation of taste between 1910, when nearly every educated person in England at least tried to read Goethe, and 1925, when very few did; the onslaught on 'Victorianism' and the deliberate erosion of romantic and post-romantic sensibility in the circles around Hulme, Pound and Wyndham Lewis; and the diminishing appeal of German idealist philosophy. Peacock has no difficulty in showing, moreover, that Eliot's hostility to Goethe was shared by many of the writers in the vanguard of

[5] Walter Muschg, *Studien zur tragischen Literaturgeschichte*, Bern 1965.

[6] Ronald Peacock; 'T.S. Eliot on Goethe', in *The Discontinuous Tradition: Studies in German Literature in honour of Ernest Ludwig Stahl*, ed. P.F. Ganz, Oxford 1971, pp. 67-78.

German Modernism — by Expressionists who exalted Kleist above Goethe; and that Eliot's remarks on Goethe occur in the course of a chapter in which Shelley and Keats are contrasted, to their disadvantage, with poets like Dante and Lucretius who (it is alleged) were content to work within existing philosophies and did not set up as philosophers on their own account.

Amidst this non-awarding of prizes to some eminent poets the offence to Goethe loses a good deal of its sting. At least, setting the statement in its context both of Eliot's general argument about the use of poetry, and about specifically romantic views of poetry, it is divested of its surface craziness; it is totally inadequate to Goethe as an estimate of the poet, but deriving logically from Eliot's own creative ideals and his own position in the poetic movement of the second and third decades of this century, it makes sense.[7]

Peacock concludes his essay with a glance at the *amende honorable* Eliot tried to make to Goethe when he accepted the Hanseatic Goethe Prize in 1954, and demonstrates that this was prompted less by a deeper understanding of Goethe or a closer relationship to his work than by a change in Eliot's thinking about the relationship of poetry to philosophy.

Peacock's contribution to 'reception' studies, born out of intimate acquaintance with the literature and intellectual climate of England and Germany, may stand for many others. It could be supplemented by studies that describe a single author's continuing preoccupation with one particular work in another language and try to trace the reasons for such preoccupation, and possibly its effects. Examples that spring to mind are Mark Twain and *Don Quixote*, Henry James and *Madame Bovary*, Tolstoy and *King Lear*, or Rilke and Baudelaire's 'carcase' poem *Une Charogne* — a poem which helped Rilke to come to terms, in his own way, with the ugly and terrible in literature as in life. But in all such confrontations two principles hold good. The first of these has been well enunciated by Donald Fanger:

We need to see [each author] on his own ground and in his own national tradition before trying to define his place in the European tradition.[8]

---

[7] Peacock, op. cit., p. 73.

[8] Donald Fanger, *Dostoevsky and Romantic Realism: A Study of Dostoevsky in Relation to Balzac, Dickens and Gogol*, Cambridge, Mass., 1965.

The second principle is that 'reception' studies and studies of 'effect' or 'influence' must go together.

'Effects' derive from living forces that have power to bring about a metamorphosis. The goal of comparative study cannot be solely to show what were, say, the European or oriental sources that Goethe used in composing his *West-Eastern Divan* — what he borrows, where he deviates and so on. That is only a preliminary collection of material. The aim should be, rather, to demonstrate the specific way in which Goethe made this traditional material his own; and — conversely — the way in which the language of Goethe's later work was affected by his sources. *Wirkung* [= effect] and *Rezeption* are processes that depend on and supplement each other.[9]

Closely linked to 'literary relation' and 'reception' studies are studies of the nature and function of *agents littéraires* or international mediators. This is part of a branch of investigation whose importance is coming to be realized more and more clearly in our own day: that of *communications*, defined by Raymond Williams as 'the institutions and forms in which ideas, information and attitudes are transmitted and received'.[10] In literary history, communication-studies may usefully begin with the sort of bird's-eye view of 'the great travel routes of thought and literature' which T.R. Henn has sketched onto the map of Europe in *The Apple and the Spectroscope*:

If you look at the map of Europe that is before you, you can see the great travel routes of thought and literature swinging northwards from the Mediterranean — Egypt to Greece; Palestine to Greece; Greece to Sicily; Sicily northwards to Rome. In Rome the eddy circles for a while, and then, by some queer trick, goes underground to rise again in Constantinople, which preserves, miraculously, what is left of both Roman and Hellenic civilization. Constantinople in its turn falls to the Turkish invaders, and the current follows the trade route up the Adriatic to North Italy, to found there the classical humanism which is to determine, by and large, the thought of Europe for the next four hundred years. From North Italy it goes up the Rhone Valley, the traditional highway for culture, or trade, or war, to Paris: spreading as it goes, both east and west. And here it is joined by a wide circling current, which has flowed from Arabia and Egypt, through Morocco,

---

[9] Horst Rüdiger, 'Nationalliteraturen und europäische Literatur', in *Definitionen: Essays zur Literatur*, ed. A. Frisé, Frankfurt 1963, p. 47.

[10] Raymond Williams, *Communications*, Harmondsworth 1962, p. 9.

across the straits to Spain, and thus across into France, into North
Italy. It is that of the Arabic Commentators on Aristotle, and the
mathematical and physical studies preserved and developed by the
Moorish civilization. It crosses to England: moving, as it were, in
rhythmic impulses of its current, impulses which are given by political
events, or the breaching of dams by the efforts of single men: scholars,
reformers, princes.

For a time the tide flows strongly in the one direction, bringing to us
nearly everything on which our traditions, and even our civilization, are
based. We may remind ourselves of some of them: the Christian
tradition, itself absorbing and consolidating what was most stable in
Hebraic and Hellenic thought; science, mathematics, and astronomy
from Egypt, Arabia, Greece; law and the science of government from
Rome; painting from Italy; architecture from that curious eddy in
Northern France which we call the Gothic. In three successive centuries
these waves of thought reach England, all, or nearly all, from the south:
following, as always, the routes of trade.[11]

Henn goes on to consider the 'strange and complicated'
native traditions which blended with such influences from
afar, and adds a necessary warning:

This, perhaps, for the broadest picture; remembering that every
generalization is valid only for so long as it takes us to examine the
parts more closely and to perceive, as we must do, the imprecision of
the first outline. That, in literary history, is an inevitable process.[12]

The simple lines of the sketch-maps Henn supplies (on
pp. 101 and 115 of his book) permit a useful first orientation; they have to be replaced by something more complex
and elaborate as one comes to appreciate more clearly the
nature of that 'continuous and extremely civilized dialogue'
which Graham Hough has seen as 'the very substance of the
English literary tradition'.

Of course the English poetic tradition has been from the start a matter
of continual influence from Latin culture — mostly from France but
nearly as much from Italy. Often a native growth has been opposed by
a highly authoritative influence from abroad, and the two have had to
be reconciled in a new synthesis. One thinks of the problem Dryden
and the neo-classic critics had in reconciling the presence of Shakespeare with the formal ideals of drama derived from France. But then

---

[11] Henn, op. cit., London 1951, pp. 99-100.

[12] ibid., p. 102.

Shakespeare himself would be unthinkable without the great body of
Romance literature from which he drew much of his material. And so it
has always gone on.[13]

In our own century, Hough adds, the pace of communication
has become more frenzied; and he contrasts a mediator like
Dryden with one like Ezra Pound who, in theory and
practice, 'neglects all the slow, thorough absorption that is
necessary for a real education', and would substitute 'a huge,
barbaric, indigestible meal of gobbets'.[14] The point is not
without its relevance for those who plan university courses in
Comparative Literature.

In drawing our own map of literary communications, we
cannot afford to neglect the itinerary and repertoire of actors
and travelling showmen. One thinks of the *Englische
Comödianten*, a troupe of players who spread some knowledge of Shakespeare's plays throughout Germany in the
seventeenth century; or the *Phantasmagoria* shows, given in
late eighteenth- and early nineteenth-century Europe by
'Robertson' (= Etienne Gaspard Robert, 1763-1837). In
Theatre Notebook[15] J.E. Varey has given accounts of
Robertson's performances in Paris, Bordeaux and Madrid,
and has demonstrated the way these animated magic lantern
shows, with their contrasts between light and darkness, their
sudden movement of the images towards or away from the
audience, fostered or reinforced in sophisticated and
unsophisticated audiences alike a taste for Gothic novels and
Night Thoughts poetry:

Many of the scenes are 'distractions funèbres', where bats, skulls and
skeletons flit across the screen or suddenly appear above the heads of
the audience. 'Jeunes beautés . . . ' cried a newspaper article describing
Robertson's performances, 'venez respirer l'air des tombeaux, vous
entretenir avec le plaintif *Young* et le sombre *Hervey*, et payer le tribut
à l'anglomanie.' Young's *Night Thoughts* appear indeed to have been
one of the principal sources of Robertson's atmosphere: the tomb, the
dejected lover, the melancholy juxtaposition of young love and death

---

[13] Graham Hough, *Image and Experience: Studies in a Literary Revolution*,
London 1960, p. 71.

[14] op. cit., p. 72.

[15] J.E. Varey, 'Robertson's Phantasmagoria in Madrid, 1821', *Theatre Notebook*,
vol. IX, no. 4, pp. 89-95, and vol. XI, no. 3, pp. 1-10.

are often the key elements in his scenes. Opposed to the scenes of graveyard melancholy, or, rather, complementary to them, was an emphasis on sentimental love, as exemplified in *Le rêve, L'offrande à l'amour* and *La naissance de l'amour champêtre*. A third feature of Robertson's repertoire was his interest in the exotic.[16]

Enid Starkie has shown[17] how important a role Michel Saint-Denis played in mediating between the French and English theatrical traditions from 1929 to the years just after the Second World War; and there can be little doubt that in our own day the itinerary of the Royal Shakespeare Company would repay similar investigation. The Polish critic Jan Kott recently testified to the seminal influence of Peter Brook's production of *Titus Andronicus*, which was brought to Warsaw in 1957, on his own thinking about Shakespeare; the views Jan Kott developed from this impetus, and from that of Brecht's theatre, in their turn influenced English attitudes to Shakespeare. For good or ill, Clifford Williams's all-male production of *As You Like It* at the Old Vic, and Peter Brook's productions of *King Lear* and *A Midsummer Night's Dream* at the Stratford Memorial Theatre and the Aldwych, owed many of their most striking features to Kott's book *Shakespeare Our Contemporary*.

The development of the radio and television play yields its investigator many similar instances of reciprocal relation — the *Hörspiel* or radio play, which has been most intensively cultivated in Germany, looks back for its origin to a little play by Richard Hughes, first broadcast by the B.B.C. on 15 January 1924 and then, in German translation, by Radio Hamburg in August 1925. And one need hardly stress that the cinema and television have proved far more powerful lines of communication than Robertson's *Phantasmagoria* ever was: so much so that in *Les Influences étrangères sur la littérature francaise (1550-1880)*, Philippe Van Tieghem is led to ask: 'Has the American novel really exerted an influence on the French novel, or have both been influenced by the cinema at the same time?'[18] What Van Tieghem

---

[16] Varey, op. cit., vol. XI, pp. 9-10.

[17] Starkie, *From Gautier to Eliot*, ed. cit., pp. 207-9.

[18] Van Tieghem, op. cit., Paris 1967, p. 248.

isolates here is the levelling effect of the cinema: affecting
two literatures at the same time, it makes it appear as though
one were influencing the other. But the cinema also, of
course, leads to the diffusion of the knowledge of other
literatures through the well-known desire to read 'the book
of the film' — English versions of Thomas Mann's *Death in
Venice* sold more briskly after the showing of Visconti's film
than before. One suspects that French and Spanish audiences
around 1820 were no less eager to seek out Lewis's *The
Monk* and Young's *Night Thoughts* — 'the book of the
phantasmagoria' — after being so delightfully frightened and
harrowed at one of Robertson's performances.

Mediators between literatures of different countries will
often be travellers, like Henry Crabb Robinson who visited
Weimar in the age of Goethe and brought back to England
tidings of the important and exciting things that were going
on there; or, slightly earlier, Georg Christoph Lichtenberg,
who mediated in the opposite direction. They may also be
diplomats of a literary turn of mind, like Eugène-Melchior de
Vogüé, Secretary of the French embassy in St. Petersburg
from 1876 to 1882, who made Russian literature known in
France with almost missionary zeal — he thought the Russian
novel particularly well qualified to deflect French literature
from what he considered the false course on which Flaubert
had set it.

I am convinced that the influence of the great Russian writers will be
salutary for our worn-out art; it will aid it to take flight again, to
observe the real better, while looking further away, and above all to
rediscover emotion. We already see something of a totally new moral
value slipping into novelistic works [. . .][19]

All these are one-way mediations; but the history of
literature also records many instances of two-way mediation.
A particularly instructive case of this latter kind is that of
Matthew Gregory Lewis ('Monk' Lewis, 1775-1818), whose
importance to the comparatist has been rightly stressed by

[19] From E.-M. de Vogüé's Preface to *Le Roman russe*, Paris 1886, p. liv. The
translation comes from George J. Becker, *Documents of Modern Literary
Realism*, Princeton 1963, p. 342.

K.S. Guthke in an excellently documented study.[20]

Lewis was born in London and educated at Westminster School, at Oxford and at Weimar (where he met Goethe). In his youth he steeped himself in the 'Gothic' horror-fictions of his time. These included Horace Walpole's *The Castle of Otranto*, with its flight from rationalism and empiricism into dreams nourished by antiquarian interests:

Visions, you know, have always been my pasture [...], and I almost think there is no wisdom comparable to that of exchanging what is called the realities of life for dreams. Old castles, old pictures, old histories, and the babble of old people, make me live back into centuries that cannot disappoint one. One holds fast and surely what is past.[21]

and Mrs. Radcliffe's *The Mysteries of Udolpho*, that masterpiece of the 'explained supernatural' of which Coleridge said: 'The reader experiences in perfection the strange luxury of artificial terror without being obliged for a moment to hoodwink his reason, or to yield to the weakness of superstitious credulity.'[22] In Germany, Lewis then came into contact with another type of literary terror: tales in which the supernatural was not comfortably distanced or explained; ballads in which man was depicted as poised between the familiar natural world and something outer-worldly or other-worldly, as constantly endangered by super-rational or sub-rational powers that often overwhelmed him. Lewis collected translations and variations of such ballads in his *Tales of Terror* and *Tales of Wonder* – and he used similar motifs, culled from Spiess's *Dwarf Peter* [*Das Petermännchen*], Musäus's *Popular Tales* [*Volksmärchen*] and the German library-fodder of the day, to produce a new type of horror-novel, in which the supernatural was linked to the darker urges of man's mind and neither 'explained' in the manner of Mrs. Radcliffe nor comfortably 'distanced' in the manner of Horace Walpole. *Ambrosio, or The Monk*, first

[20] K.S. Guthke, *Englische Vorromantik und deutscher Sturm und Drang: M.G. Lewis' Stellung in der Geschichte der deutsch-englischen Literaturbeziehungen*, Göttingen 1958.

[21] Horace Walpole to George Montague, 5.1.1766.

[22] *Monthly Review*, 1794.

published in 1795, brought elements of German pre-romanticism and sub-romanticism into the English novel and decisively influenced English taste in such matters. Words-worth's recoil from the results of that influence is well-known. At the same time, however, Lewis's *Monk* had a great vogue in Germany, where it strengthened the irrationalism and sensationalism already present and mingled these with the atmospheric suggestiveness Lewis had derived from Mrs. Radcliffe, as well as a carnality which was Lewis's own special contribution to the 'Gothic' genre. Many features of *Ambrosio, or The Monk* reappear in E.T.A. Hoffmann's one completed novel, *The Devil's Elixirs;*[23] and Hoffmann acknowledged his debt by allowing one of his central characters to read, at a decisive turn in her fortunes, Lewis's shudder-provoking tale. What Hoffmann learnt from Lewis then worked its way into the literatures of France[24] and Russia, where Hoffmann's works were translated and eagerly read in the course of the nineteenth century. Elements from the Gothic novel found their way into the work of Dostoevsky, for instance, through at least three different mediators: through Hoffmann, through Balzac, and through Dickens.

Mediators or *agents littéraires* need not, as the case of de Vogüé has shown, themselves be writers of imaginative literature. They can be great translators and scholars like Arthur Waley, the chief intermediary, in our own time, between European and Far Eastern letters, to whom Brecht owes no less a debt than Ezra Pound; or Robert Lowth, the Oxford Professor of Poetry in the mid-eighteenth century, whose contacts with Professor J.D. Michaelis of Göttingen benefited German literary theory and literary practice. Lowth tried to understand Biblical poetry better by going to the countries in which it originated and studying the civilizations that survived there or of which traces could still be found; Michaelis found his own tentative advances in the same direction encouraged and corrected by Lowth's books

[23] *Die Elixiere des Teufels*, 1815-16.

[24] There are also, of course, traces of Lewis's direct influence on French literature and sub-literature. The *Journal de Paris* opined in 1810: 'There is no name in the history of the novel more famous than that of M. Lewis. (Guthke, op. cit., p. 178).

and letters. What began with the Bible was soon extended to the Homeric epics. Robert Wood, like Lowth, tried to see the 'originality' of the ancients against the particular conditions they encountered in their world and their time; he too travelled to the places the poet must have known, searching for relics of his civilization among the people that still lived there as well as in documents and artistic records of the past. Wood's *Essay on the Original Genius of Homer* was published in London in 1759; and once again J.D. Michaelis constituted himself the chief spokesman in Germany of the English scholar's views. Through Michaelis Herder and Goethe came to hear of these studies; and through Herder and Goethe they had the most profound effect on that conception of 'original genius' and its links with a particular civilization which became so characteristic of the German Storm and Stress movement. It is no accident, of course, that it should have been a professor in Göttingen who mediated in this way between England and Germany: for as the university town of Hanover, Göttingen had a special connection with England under the Hanoverian dynasty.[25]

As this example should have demonstrated, a *place*, with the right person in it, can act as an important agent in international literary exchanges; so can a whole country, like Switzerland,[26] or a region, like Alsace; and so, of course, can a firm or an institution. Here the printing-presses have played an important part. John L. Lievsay has shown how energetic English printers of the sixteenth and seventeenth centuries helped to bring the language and literature of Italy into England and helped to create the Englishman's appetite for things Italian;[27] and in more recent times, the role of enterprising publishers as well as radio and television can hardly be over-estimated. Special interest attaches also to the great international literary journals which often published works in more than one language: Herwarth Walden's *Sturm*

[25] cf. Hans Hecht, *T. Percy, R. Wood und J.D. Michaelis: Ein Beitrag zur Literaturgeschichte der Genieperiode*, Stuttgart 1933.

[26] A book by Fritz Ernst, published in 1939, bears the telling title: *Helvetia mediatrix*.

[27] John L. Lievsay, *The Englishman's Italian Books 1550-1700*, Philadelphia 1969.

in Berlin, important as an organ of Italian Futurism, German
Expressionism, and the beginnings of French Surrealism; E.
Osvát's *Nyugat*, which sought to 'Westernise' Hungarian
literature before the First World War; and Eugene Jolas's
transition, founded in the late 1920s. Jolas, as Malcolm
Cowley had pointed out in *Exile's Return*,[28] seemed pre-
destined for his role as cultural mediator: born in New
Jersey, he was transported back in early childhood to his
family's home in French-speaking Lorraine, then under the
German flag; he attended German schools before joining his
American relatives in Iowa; he became a journalist in America
and made contact with many writers there; between 1922
and 1925, and again in 1926, he worked as a reporter in
France. After an early period of eclecticism, in which
Futurist exaltations of machinery appeared cheek-by-jowl
with anti-mechanistic and anti-technological writings, Jolas's
transition, founded in Paris in 1927, worked itself towards a
policy of its own that combined what Cowley has described
as its editor's three principal preoccupations: Rimbaud
(hallucination of the senses), Joyce (linguistic and structural
experiments) and Surrealism (emphasis on dreams and
'autonomous' imaginative processes). Jolas printed translations and discussions of German, Russian and French
experimental writing side by side with Joyce's *Work in
Progress*; he thus helped to bring about the confluence of
various European and American 'modernisms'. Experimenting
authors could find confirmation, and suggestions for new ways
of writing, by seeing their own work alongside that of writers
from other countries.[29]

In our own day, a somewhat different kind of confluence
is being encouraged by journals like *Black Orpheus, Abbia,
African Arts/Arts d'Afrique* and *Présence Africaine*, which
bring together writings of authors whose native African
dialects have influenced their use of European Languages
(English, French and Portuguese). They are helping to create

---

[28] Malcolm Cowley, *Exile's Return*, New York 1934, 2nd (revised) ed. 1951.

[29] cf. J.M. Ritchie's paper on 'Translations of the German Expressionists in
Eugene Jolas's journal *transition*'; summary to be printed in the *Acta* of the XIIth
International Congress of the International Federation for Modern Languages and
Literatures, held at Cambridge in 1972.

a new multi-lingual African literature whose blending of African with European modes and themes has already produced works worthy of serious attention. Here a rich field is being opened up to comparatists prepared to acquire knowledge of traditional forms of poetry and story-telling in Africa, and investigate the marriage of these with European forms in the work of such writers as Senghor, Dadié, Soyinka, Achebe, Onologuem, or Oyono.

The subject of 'communications', it need hardly be stressed, offers particular scope to sociologists and cultural historians; and these too will find themselves, again and again, widening their perspectives to include writers in more than one language. When Robert Escarpit, for instance, tries to construct a typology of literary distribution, he cites a Japanese example at one end of the scale — the *yomiuri*, at once authors, advertisers and distributors of literary works — and a predominantly American example at the other: vast publishing, printing, advertising and distributing complexes which even, for certain types of production, include authors among their salaried staff.[30]

In assessing literary mediation before the twentieth century, one must beware of overestimating its speed and effectiveness. Lilian Furst makes this point forcibly in her study of the relation between German and French Romanticism:

Since the spread of new ideas was largely dependent on the chance reports of travellers in an age when communications were still relatively poor and further disrupted by war, information on contemporary developments even in neighbouring countries was often scant and belated, so that many assumptions of influence must be discounted. The outstanding example of such slow and fragmentary infiltration of ideas is to be found in [Mme de Staël's] *De l'Allemagne*: though written by a perspicacious and widely-travelled critic, it contains in 1810 very few of the ideas of the Jena Romantics which were to reach France only some half a century later.[31]

---

[30] R. Escarpit, 'Succès et survie littéraires', in *Le Littéraire et le social: Eléments pour une sociologie de la littérature*, Paris 1970, p. 130.

[31] Lilian Furst, *Romanticism in Perspective: A Comparative Study of Aspects of the Romantic Movements in England, France and Germany*, London 1969, p. 51. The case of Mme de Staël is, of course, complicated by her polemical purposes. She had, in fact, as her constant literary adviser, one of the men who had helped to shape the ideas of the Jena Romantics: A.W. Schlegel.

One must also, when studying the work of literary mediators, guard against falling victim to the fallacy of the single factor. Many historical, social and economic forces may help or hinder mediation; many men and women may work separately or together, consciously or unconsciously, to the same end. Shakespeare's triumph in eighteenth-century Germany, and the creation of *unser Shakespeare* in the Romantic period, were prepared by Lichtenberg's reports of Garrick's London performances, Wieland's and Eschenburg's translations, Heufeld's adaptations for the Austrian stage, Schröder's work as an actor-manager in Hamburg, Lessing's polemic against Gottsched, Herder's literary criticism and philosophy of history, and others too numerous to list. This is not to deny, of course, that the decisive impetus may frequently come from a single book — even an indifferent one like Arthur Symons's *The Symbolist Movement in Literature* (1889), which inspired some of the leading poets of the English-speaking world to look more closely at what had been happening in French poetry, and to discover its relevance to their own work. Nor must it be forgotten that sister-arts have often played an important part in stimulating interest in and diffusion of a country's literature abroad. Interest in African sculpture led to interest in African literature; Surrealist painting made the diffusion of Dada and Surrealist anti-literature easier; and the great German composers mediated, throughout the world, a first acquaintance with the work of Goethe and Mörike, Eichendorff and Heine — and, of course, with Schiller's *Ode to Joy*, whose ironic presence in Anthony Burgess's *A Clockwork Orange* is due entirely to Beethoven. Richard Wagner especially, as Werner Vordtriede has demonstrated,[32] proved a powerful mediator between German Romanticism and French writers and affected the form as well as the content of French literature.

Study of 'literary mediation' needs to be combined, on occasions, with that of paradigm cases: with the study of authors whose reading and writing show with particular clarity what it was a given society, or segment of society,

[32] Werner Vordtriede, *Novalis und die französischen Symbolisten.* Stuttgart 1963.

found in literary works that came to it from abroad. Graham Hough has investigated such a paradigm case in his essay on 'George Moore and the Nineties'. Moore, he tells us,

was more completely involved in French literature than any other writer of the nineties — more even than Symons; and we can see in him a complete microcosm of the French influences that were then reshaping English literature. His experience tells us of the opening of a new chapter in the history of English fiction. Three steady preoccupations can be discerned among his shifting allegiances: one is with telling the truth about experience instead of merely devising an agreeable story; the second is with imaginative freedom in spite of the circulating libraries and the young ladies; the third is with formal justness and beauty, in expression and organisation, instead of the laboured or slapdash approximations to which the English novel in all but its highest moments had been prone. Together they make a break with many of the traditions of English fiction — with the traditions of picaresque adventure, indiscriminate humour, genial satire and reforming zeal. A severer artistic ideal takes their place. And this break is not merely a matter of Moore's own work [. . .] The lessons he was learning were also being learnt, wholly or in part, by Hardy, Conrad and Henry James.[33]

The case of Moore is particularly instructive, because it shows so clearly how writers working in England managed to fuse what would have seemed conflicting tendencies: Zola and Gautier, the realist-naturalist mode and the symbolist-aesthetic.

Investigations of the kind described in this chapter have not infrequently been attacked even by those who in other respects champion the cause of comparative literary studies. Anthony Thorlby, for instance, in a *Times Literary Supplement* article reprinted in the *Yearbook of Comparative and General Literature* for 1968, complains that the study of 'so-called "international" influences, that is, the reception and reputation of an author in some country other than his own' indicates 'a largely second-hand interest in original authors and works', and turns all too frequently 'into rather artificial surveys, where the interest of what is established is minimal in comparison with the labour of research'.[34] But

[33] Graham Hough, *Image and Experience: Studies in a Literary Revolution*, London 1960, pp. 196-7.

[34] Anthony Thorlby, *Yearbook of Comparative and General Literature* XVII (1968), p. 76.

Thorlby himself admits that a scholar like Baldensperger or Wellek can make a book of this kind the occasion for exceptional insights into the mind both of the writer whose reputation is being considered, and those he influenced. It cannot be unimportant to study the way literature passes into history, acts in the social world, or establishes and breaks through forms and conventions.

> If literary creation [. . .] bridges the 'gap' between historical experience and the poem as between two different 'orders' of the real, by a kind of displacement of experience, the career of the book represents, and is a function of, the replacement of the poem in history. This branch of comparative studies contributes significantly, I think, to the theory of literary history.[35]

Here as elsewhere it is important, of course, to have an eye for what is significant and not to mistake quantity for quality:

> [The] tendency to concentrate on the external facts of cultural exchange (translations, travellers' reports, reviews, periodicals, etc.) can lead to [a] very real pitfall: the temptation to deduce from the sheer quantity of such contact between various literatures the presence of an interaction decisive in quality. But the mere existence of even a considerable number of translations and personal links need not inevitably result in any profound reciprocal effect.[36]

The book from which this warning comes, and the studies by Asselineau, Eliot, Peacock, Hough, Gundolf and Guthke examined in the present chapter, may serve to demonstrate that an interest in 'literary fortunes' and 'mediation' need not — and, indeed, must not — go with a refusal to submit oneself to first-hand experience of literary works.

---

[35] Claudio Guillén, *Literature as System: Essays toward the Theory of Literature*, Princeton 1971, p. 49.

[36] Lilian Furst, *Romanticism in Perspective: A Comparative Study of Aspects of the Romantic Movement in England, France and Germany*, ed. cit., p. 15.

4.
Influence, Analogy and Tradition

The study of literary relations, communications and international mediators, discussed in the previous chapter, cannot be divorced from the investigation of 'influences'; and that, of course, brings us into the most hotly disputed area in the whole realm of comparative studies — a realm often transformed into a battle-field by opposing scholars. Simon Jeune sees 'influence' study as the very centre of Comparative Literature:

Comparative Literature studies, essentially, the influence authors, or the literatures of different nations, have exerted on one another, as well as the diffusion of such influences. The national point of departure is never allowed out of sight, and these studies often go into minute particulars.[1]

— while René Wellek condemns the whole enterprise of studying literary relations and influences as irremediably tainted by an unreflecting positivism:

The organized enterprise of comparative literature in France accomplished mainly an enormous accumulation of evidence about literary relations, particularly on the history of reputations, the intermediaries between nations — travellers, translators, and propagandists. The unexamined assumption in such research is the existence of a neutral fact which is supposed to be connected as if by a thread with other preceding facts. But the whole conception of a 'cause' in literary study is singularly uncritical; nobody has ever been able to show that a work of art was 'caused' by another work of art, even though parallels and similarities can be accumulated. A later work of art may not have been possible without a preceding one, but it cannot have been caused by it.[2]

---

[1] Simon Jeune, *Littérature générale et littérature comparée*, Paris 1968, p. 39.

[2] René Wellek, *Discriminations*, Yale University Press 1970, p. 35.

In the last-quoted sentence Wellek has, however, it seems to me, himself provided a rationale for diachronic comparative study. What *is* there in the earlier work which made it 'possible' for the later to be produced? In what way did the later work build on (and modify) ground prepared by the earlier one? What expectations aroused by the earlier work did the later disappoint or satisfy? It is these questions which meaningful 'influence' studies seek to answer.

A. Owen Aldridge, in a useful anthology, has recently reminded us that questions of 'influence' cannot be divorced from questions of 'analogy', 'affinity' and 'tradition'; it is therefore important, before assessing the role of 'influence' studies in comparative literature, to survey, briefly, the related fields just mentioned. Aldridge defined 'analogy' or 'affinity' as 'resemblances in style, structure, mood or idea between works which have no other connection'.[3] He seems to have in mind two main kinds of studies. The first of these may be exemplified by the work of James J.Y. Liu, who, in several books on poetry, chivalrous tradition and dramatic conventions, has drawn parallels between the literatures of China and of Europe. One of Liu's studies, *Elizabethan and Yuan*,[4] has become particularly well-known because René Etiemble used it as a key-example in his widely-read, provocatively titled book on the 'crisis' of Comparative Literature, *Comparaison n'est pas raison*.[5] Plays from the Far East were not known in Elizabethan England, yet Liu is able to show that the two kinds of drama he examined had certain conventions in common. Both were anti-illusionist, both were equally remote from the kind of drama Liu described as 'a *slice of life* as lived by Mr. Smith and Mr. Jones in his drawing-room with the fourth wall missing'. It is precisely the *lack* of mutual influence which makes the comparison interesting and meaningful to Etiemble and to others who want to study the inherent possibilities of drama and the

[3] A. Owen Aldridge, *Comparative Literature: Matter and Method*, Urbana 1969, p. 3.

[4] James J.Y. Liu, *Elizabethan and Yuan: A Brief Comparison of Some Conventions in Poetic Drama*, London 1955.

[5] René Etiemble, *Comparaison n'est pas raison: La crise de la littérature comparée*, Paris 1963.

processes by which life is transformed into certain forms of art. No study of this kind will, however, quite fit Aldridge's definition. There is always some 'other connection' beside the 'resemblance in style, structure, mood or idea' — in the case just cited authors in both countries were (to put it no higher) writing for the stage, and a stage without naturalistic decor at that.

The other main kind of 'affinity' or 'analogy' study may be illustrated from the work of the German scholar H.R. Jauss. In an essay on the literary revolution at the end of the Age of Goethe,[6] Jauss analyses the concept of the grotesque expounded in Hugo's *Préface de Cromwell* (1827), and shows how this differs from earlier notions of the grotesque as 'bizarre', 'burlesque', 'extravagant', as well as from Romantic notions that equate the grotesque with the 'uncanny' and see it as a sign of another order of being breaking into our ordered world. In the *Préface de Cromwell* the grotesque is a step towards the depiction of reality, *le réel*: towards recognizing the existence in this world of mixtures of the sublime, the ugly and the ridiculous which the doctrine of segregated levels of style tried to keep out of literature. In his defence of allowing such mixtures to enter literature, Hugo cites prominently Napoleon's saying: 'Du sublime au ridicule il n'y a qu'un pas'[7] — a saying which is also of central importance in Heine's *Ideas: The Book of Le Grand* [*Ideen: Das Buch LeGrand*] , published at about the same time as the *Préface de Cromwell* and clearly independent of it. Hugo's demand for a 'mélange du sublime et du grotesque' finds its parallel in Heine's demand for combining the grand gestures that go with a grand style (*das Pathetische*) with comic elements. In both cases there is revolt against a view of literature that would neatly divide works whose subject and effect are 'grotesque' or 'comic' from others whose subject and effect are 'sublime' or 'tragic' — in both cases this demand for subversion and mingling in literature is made in

[6] H.R. Jauss, 'Das Ende der Kunstperiode — Aspekte der literarischen Revolution bei Heine, Hugo and Stendhal', in *Literaturgeschichte als Provokation*, Frankfurt 1970, pp. 67-106.

[7] 'It is only a step from the sublime to the ridiculous.'

the name of emotional truth, and in both cases it may be linked to social and political upheavals. Jauss speaks, provocatively, of a 'July Revolution in literature'.

No less interesting than the likenesses are the differences Jauss detects. Heine's faith in providential or ultimate reconciliation of the discords signalled by the grotesque is much weaker than that of Hugo; and these differences have clear connections with the different ways in which the art of Hugo and that of Heine were to develop. Once again, however, one cannot say, with Aldridge, that there is no 'other connection' than those of 'style, structure, mood or idea'. In the case of Heine and Hugo the connections are clear: similar experience of history and society, and a similar feeling that a classical or classicizing aesthetic was inadequate to portray the realities of the nineteenth century. In an investigation like that of Jauss the critic does not so much compare two works with each other as see them both against a similar historical and social background, measure them against the 'parameters' of European historical and social processes.

The approach of H.R. Jauss and his pupils is close to that which has been advocated by some Marxist historians of literature, particularly V.M. Zhirmunsky. Zhirmunsky has investigated several literary analogies or parallels in which there has been no contact or direct influence — between the concept of the hero in French *chansons de geste*, for instance, and that in Russian folk-ballads; he has sought to account for these by pointing to similarities in the social structure of the groups within which these 'historical-typological analogies' came into being.

The comparative study of these common trends of literary evolution leads to a comprehension of some of the general laws of literary development and of the social preconditions, and at the same time to an understanding of the historical and national peculiarity of each individual literature.[8]

C.L. Wrenn, who quotes this passage in *The Idea of*

---

[8] W.M. Zhirmunsky, 'On the Study of Comparative Literature', *Oxford Slavonic Papers* 13 (1967), p. 2.

Comparative Literature,[9] adds that this typological approach
has proved fruitful in *Beowulf* studies and points to its
affinities with the methods and presuppositions of the
Chadwicks' *The Growth of Literature.* Western critics can
thus learn from Zhirmunsky, even if they do not believe,
with Zhirmunsky's East European disciples and successors,
that 'comprehension of the general laws of literary development and of the social preconditions' implies acceptance of a
Marxist-Leninist model of historical development.

Literary analogies that may be referred, in part at least, to
similar social and political processes, are observable in many
fields: a recent example would be the spontaneous generation
of 'Dada' phenomena in Europe and the U.S.A. during the
First World War. The 'anti-literature' and 'anti-art' demonstrations of the group about Man Ray and Marcel Duchamp
in New York strikingly paralleled the demonstrations organized independently in Zürich by Hugo Ball, Tristan Tzara,
Marcel Janco and others. Both were to some extent, of
course, influenced by Italian Futurism, as were also the
Russian Futurists who evolved their *'zaum'* sound-poetry at
about the same time as, and independently of, Hugo Ball; but
the parallels do suggest similar historical 'parameters', and
look as though they were a common response, by intellectuals in Europe and the U.S.A., to the situation in which
art and artists found themselves at the outbreak of the First
World War.

Two other kinds of 'analogy' studies deserve mention. The
first of these is the investigation of strikingly similar *images*
and *image-complexes* that turn up in the work of poets who
had no contact with one another: the image of the 'black
sun', for instance, in Blake and Nerval. For such similarities
critics have frequently sought a Jungian interpretation — they
have been seen as archetypes given within the structure of the
human imagination. Gilbert Durand's ambitious surveys of
the 'anthropological structure' of imaginative literature[10]

---

[9] Presidential address published by the Modern Humanities Research Association,
Leeds 1968. The quotation from Zhirmunsky, and Wrenn's comment, appear on
p. 20.

[10] Especially *Les Structures anthropologiques de l'imaginaire: Introduction à
l'archétypologie générale*, Grenoble 1960.

attempt nothing less than a phenomenology of the imagination, with as yet very questionable results.

The other area of 'analogy' studies that must not go
unmentioned is that which undertakes the study of a given
theme in a given literary genre all over the world. This has
produced at least one classic: *EOS: An Enquiry into the
Theme of Lovers' Meetings and Partings at Dawn in Poetry*
– a volume in which many scholars had a hand and which
was edited and introduced by Arthur Hatto.[11] Hatto and his
collaborators show how the theme identified in the sub-title
has been treated by primitive and sophisticated poets,
literally from China to Peru, from earliest times to the times
of Shakespeare. Many of the striking analogies that appear in
these studies may, of course, be traced to common human
experience, and to the consequences that flow from any
attempt to mould the raw material of life into the formal
perfection of the lyric poet's art. There is interplay, here,
between the three main factors that make for typological
analogies: *social* (two societies may have reached a similar
stage of development or find themselves faced with similar
problems); *literary* (at certain stages of their development a
given genre may develop a dynamic of its own and lead to
similar development which then may, or may not, be
strengthened by direct contact with foreign models); and
psychological (the human mind has common ways of
responding to common experience; two authors may have a
similar cast of mind). Independent evolution, of course, does
not account for all resemblances. In his essay 'On Fairy-
stories', J.R.R. Tolkien puts into perspective the problem
faced by the contributors to *EOS* no less than by folklorists:'

We are [. . .] confronted with a variant of the problem that the
archaeologist encounters, or the comparative philologist: with the
debate between *independent evolution* (or rather *invention*) of the
similar; *inheritance* from a common ancestry; and *diffusion* at various
times from one or more centres [. . .] All three things [. . .] have
evidently played their part in producing the intricate web of Story.[12]

---

[11] *EOS: An Enquiry into the Theme of Lovers' Meetings and Partings at Dawn in
Poetry,* The Hague 1965.

[12] J.R.R. Tolkien, *Tree and Leaf*, London 1964, p. 24.

Except in a few fortunate cases, Tolkien adds, it is now 'beyond all skill but that of the elves' to unravel that web.

As *EOS* passes from consideration of folk-song in many countries to that of Provençal and Middle High German *aubades* and *tagelieder*, it necessarily merges 'analogy' studies with the study of 'tradition' — and there can be few areas of literary investigation in which the question of tradition must not sooner or later be faced. The poets themselves are conscious of this. When Shelley writes his elegy on the death of Keats, *Adonais*, he places himself deliberately into a tradition of pastoral elegy in English (whose greatest exemplar is Milton's *Lycidas*) and beyond that into the tradition of Greek and Latin pastoral elegy. When he writes a poem entitled *The Triumph of Life*, he signals by this very title that he is continuing, and varying, Petrarch's *Trionfi*; when he writes an *Ode to Heaven* or an *Ode to the West Wind* he signifies, again by his very title, that he wishes his work to be seen against the background of other English odes (those of Collins, for instance) and, of course, the classical odes of Pindar and Horace. Here is a field in which comparisons between works in different languages are vitally necessary. Dependence on and variation of traditional 'models' are signalled, especially in pre-Romantic works, by verbal reminiscences and mythological references — a tissue of allusions which has been notably analysed, in a famous instance, by Northrop Frye's 'Literature as Context: Milton's Lycidas'.[13] Tradition may, of course, figure more negatively than it does in Milton: one thinks of Heine's parody of the Greek gods, and the poetry that celebrates them, in the *North Sea* cycle, with its continual rejection of a too long venerated past. Here too, however, we must know and recognize the tradition, appreciate what is being rejected in order to understand what is being affirmed.

In the study of literary tradition the national and the international come together in characteristically complex ways. Distinguished comparatists have often shown themselves eager to enrich a particular national heritage through

---

[13] *Comparative Literature: Proceedings of the Second Congress of the I.C.L.A.*, Chapel Hill 1959, vol. I.

contact with others. Herder, for instance, when he translated and expounded the poetry of many lands, wanted to bring before his countrymen ways of treating common human themes of which they were not aware or which they despised; but he also sought to foster, *by means of international comparisons*, a specifically national, German way of writing. His essay 'On the resemblance between Middle English and German Literature'[14] tried to show how other nations — particularly the British — had drawn strength and sustenance from their own traditions of folk-song, folk-tales and popular entertainment; the reason why German literature lagged so far behind the English was the neglect, by German poets and scholars, of similar traditions in their own country. It is a tribute to the success of Herder's advocacy and Goethe's example that when a similar 'popularist' movement gathered strength in nineteenth-century Spain, it looked to Germany for its inspiration in much the same way as Germany had once looked to England. G.A. Bécquer's preface to Augusto Ferrán's *La soledad*, written in 1860, asks Spanish poets to seek inspiration from Andalusian folk-song, and quotes Goethe, Schiller, Uhland and Heine as examples of the strength sophisticated poets can draw from the popular traditions of their native country.

Studies of literary tradition involve genre-study too (of which more later), as well as investigation of *topoi*, commonplaces and a common stock of images and rhetorical devices such as those examined in Ernst Robert Curtius's *European Literature and the Latin Middle Ages*.[15] Curtius believed that he had found in medieval literature the key to a system of forms and formulae which constituted a stable element in the literary tradition from Homer to Hofmannsthal. He therefore compiled a kind of *rhetorica nova*, listing *topoi* and forms which he regarded as literary constants: situations, landscapes, ways of beginning and ending a work, metaphors. . . . He is particularly interested in the processes by which such material is transmitted from one generation and one country to another, and therefore pays welcome attention to the

---

[14] 'Von Ahnlichkeit der mittlern englischen und deutschen Dichtkunst', 1777.

[15] *Europäische Literatur und lateinisches Mittelalter*, 2nd edition, Berne 1954.

history of education, and to changing habits of reading and study. He is also aware of the many different attitudes a writer may adopt to the 'constants' he finds — these range from slavish submission to out-and-out rejection. But when all obvious media of transmission have been analysed, there still remains a puzzling phenomenon. Let us take one of Curtius's most famous instances, discussed also by Claude Pichois and André M. Rousseau[16], the *topos* of the *puer senex*, the idea of a child that has all the qualities of an old man. Curtius finds instances of this in Virgil and Cicero, in the Bible, in medieval and Renaissance literature. But the same topos can be found in Chinese graphic and literary representations, quite independently of Hebrew and Roman sources; and so Curtius finds himself driven back, in his attempts to account for *analogous* phenomena of this kind, to the Jungian idea of archetypes and (alack and alas) a collective unconscious.

Curtius's book has fathered a whole host of studies tracing the emergence, persistence and variation of various *topoi*. One of the better examples is Heinz Galinsky's book *Naturae Cursus*,[17] which follows the fortunes of just one metaphor — 'the course of nature' — from Pindar to St. Augustine, from Boëthius to Petrarch, from Wyatt to Shakespeare, from metaphysical poetry to the English Romantics and across the Atlantic to the U.S.A. (where it surfaces in the Declaration of Independence). In comparing the various contexts of the phrase, and the various metamorphoses it undergoes, Galinsky keeps in mind both the history of ideas and that of literary forms: he describes his book as *Form-, Ideen- und Funktionsgeschichte eines kleinen literarischen Gebildes.*[18] The only question that may remain in the reader's mind is whether the tracing of this metaphor through so many works in different languages has really done more than list a large number of instances; whether we understand either Shakespeare's eighteenth Sonnet or the American Declaration of Independence better because we know that an important

---

[16] In *La Littérature comparée*, 2nd edition. 1967, p. 96.

[17] Heinz Galinsky, *Naturae Cursus*, Heidelberg 1968.

[18] *A history of the forms, ideas and functions of a small literary configuration.*

image which occurs in both also occurs in Cicero.

One does not, of course, always have to begin, as Curtius and Galinsky do, with classical antiquity and the European Middle Ages. It is possible to conceive a meaningful study which traces the fortunes of one of the central images of Edgar Allan Poe's tales — that of the Manuscript found in a Bottle — in Vigny, Mallarmé and many poets of European Modernism right up to its recent use in a key-statement on his own poetic practice by an important poet writing in German: Paul Celan. This kind of study works backwards as well as forwards. In some famous lines of Verlaine's autumn poem *Chanson d'Automne:*

> Et je m'en vais
> Au vent mauvais
>   Qui m'emporte
> Deçà, delà,
> Pareil à la
>   Feuille morte,[19]

a comparatist will hear resonances going back to Dante's 'aero maligno', the evil wind of hell that sweeps the lost souls hither and thither: 'di qua, di la, di giu, di su li mena' — a passage which is itself a conscious variation on some autumnal lines in Virgil.[20]

'Influence' studies proper are perhaps the most suspect and maligned area of comparative investigation. Virginia Woolf has only to say of a character in *To the Lighthouse* that he is 'working on the influence of something on somebody' for us to know that he is remote and ineffectual and that his work is arid. In recent years, however, a brilliant defence of these studies has come from the pen of Wolfgang Clemen, to whose classifications my own typology is much indebted.[21]

First and lowliest there is the study of direct borrowing: Shakespeare and Kleist taking a plot from Plautus; Chaucer taking over stories, lines and phrases from French, Italian and

[19] And I go on my way / In the evil wind / That bears me along / Hither, thither, / Like the / Dead leaf.

[20] *Aeneid* VI, 305 ff.

[21] Wolfgang Clemen, 'Was ist literarischer Einfluss'? in *Neusprachliche Mitteilungen aus Wissenschaft und Praxis,* III (1968), pp. 139-47.

Latin poetry; Lesage and Smollett building their fiction on
the plot sub-structure of the Spanish picaresque novel; Brecht
lifting lines — even complete poems — from German translations of Villon, Rimbaud and Kipling and incorporating
these, without acknowledgement, in his plays. Noting likenesses here is an essential step to noting differences: to seeing
what ·Shakespeare or Kleist made of Plautus's plot, how
Chaucer used his French, Italian and Latin sources to enrich
the English language, how Lesage and Smollett altered the
picaresque mode, how poems and lines by Villon and
Rimbaud make a quite new and different effect in the
context of *The Threepenny Opera*. The multitude of verbal
borrowings in Chaucer, Wolfgang Clemen rightly warns us,
must not lead us to think that Chaucer was influenced by
French, Italian or Latin poetry to the extent that his
individuality was submerged. On the contrary: Chaucer's
early poems show how the mosaic of borrowings combines
into a new pattern, a new ground-plan, and new artistic
effects which we can recognize as Chaucer's own.

An excellent exemplification of the sort of analysis that is
here required — tracing the various models and traditions, the
very phrases used, to other works of literature, and then
showing that the work analysed is yet a powerfully original
whole — may be found, once again, in Dámaso Alonso's
Poesia Española. In his discussion of Fray Luis de Léon's *Ode
to Salinas*, Alonso shows in exquisite detail how three
different strands here come together: the Platonic, with its
progress from the single instance of beauty perceived here on
earth to the unchanging Idea of Beauty; the mystic, with its
elevation of the soul from contemplation of this world to
unison with God; and the formal traditions of the Horatian
ode, with its structure of climax and anti-climax, capable of
mirroring the rising of the soul implicit in the Platonic and
the mystic scheme, the overpowering but fleeting moment of
vision, and the necessary descent back to life here below. In
welding all this into an indissoluble unity, Fray Luis has
created a poem which is at once traditional and individual; a
poem which no-one at all familiar with Spanish poetry could
take for the work of any other author.

Alonso's example has in fact led us to a second type of

'influence' study which may be considered meaningful: that
of a conflux of impulses from various literatures, which join
the traditions the poet finds in his native country and
stimulate the talent he was born with. In Heine's later prose,
for instance, the techniques and materials of French historiography and political journalism are blended with others he
had found in Goethe, in A.W. Schlegel, in Börne, in 'Young
German' writings, and with forms he had evolved for himself
in his *Pictures of Travel [Reisebilder]*. Analysing how Heine
combined elements from these various 'models' into something very much his own is as useful and fascinating a study
as the investigation of what T.S. Eliot made of the work of
Baudelaire and Laforgue, whose formative influence on his
own poetry he has himself acknowledged. There are, indeed,
many important European poets who cannot be adequately
discussed with reference solely to the literary traditions of
their native languages; poets like Rilke, who learnt from
Russia and — above all — from France 'with an instinctive
and unerring ability to extract just what he needed from a
place or a person without surrendering his autonomy or being
tempted to linger longer than the process of assimilation
demanded'.[22] As the book from which I have just quoted
makes admirably clear, such influences are not confined to
literature and the spoken or written language: the work of
Rodin and Cézanne was as important a factor in the
evolution of Rilke's poetic style as that of Baudelaire and
Valéry.

The examples from Heine and Rilke lead us naturally to a
third type of 'influence' study meaningful in the context of
comparative literature: the study of literatures in contact
(French, German and Italian writing in Switzerland, for
instance) and that of the literature of exile (the effect of a
foreign ambience on the work of Heine living in Paris, or that
of Turgenev living in Paris and Baden-Baden). Malcolm
Cowley has devoted some interesting pages of *Exile's Return*
to the impact of French literature on the expatriate
American writers of the 1920s. He shows how they studied
not only Joyce and Eliot, but also — especially — Flaubert,

[22] K.A.J. Batterby, *Rilke and France: A Study of Poetic Development*, Oxford
1966, p. 106.

Proust, Gide, Rimbaud and Mallarmé:

They had more to learn from French than from English masters at the time, and moreover the French influence proved the safer for young American writers because it was in a different language. If they had studied English authors they would have become at best disciples and at worst copyists. Studying French literature, on the other hand, they had the problem of reproducing its best qualities in another language, and it led them to a difficult and fruitful search for equivalents. The language in which they tried to recreate the French qualities was not literary English but colloquial American. That was among the unexpected effects of their exile: it was in Paris that some of them, notably Ernest Hemingway, worked on the problems of transforming Midwestern speech into a medium for serious fiction. Others worked on the problem of giving a legendary quality to Southern or Midwestern backgrounds. The result of all these labours was a new literature so different from its French models that when the American writers of the lost generation became popular reading in France, as they did in the years before and after World War II, the French spoke of them as powerful, a little barbarous, and entirely original. The French critics had failed to recognize that these foreigners belonged in part to the tradition of Flaubert.[23]

If the French thus received from their American guests a gift that derived to no small extent from their own literary heritage, the Americans, in their turn, discovered in France how much use they could make of elements present in earlier American literature. As Cowley puts it:

Some qualities of the new writing had been encountered before. The careful workmanship, the calculation of effects even when the novelists seemed to be writing in a casual style, the interest in finer shades of behaviour (including abnormal behaviour), the hauntedness and the gift for telling a headlong story full of violent action — all these qualities had appeared many times in American literature, beginning with Charles Brockden Brown [. . .] and extending in different combinations through the work of Poe, Hawthorne, Melville, Henry James, Stephen Crane and many minor writers, so that they seemed to express a constant strain in the American character. Here was a tradition that had been broken for a time, but the new novelists had reestablished it, and that was perhaps the most important result of their adventure.[24]

Cowley has no difficulty in showing that the symbiotic

[23] op. cit., revised ed., New York 1951, p. 299. The book was originally published in 1934.
[24] ibid., p. 300.

process begun in Paris was continued when hundreds of European writers followed the returning American 'exiles' westward across the Atlantic: the Germans opposed to Hitler, the Spanish anti-fascists, Jewish writers of many nations, and then, when Europe was overrun, Frenchmen, Belgians, refugees from all parts of central Europe . . . . 'There was a time,' Cowley concludes, with some exaggeration, 'when New York was what Paris had been in 1920, the place where every writer wanted to be, the capital of the literary world.' The effects of their American ambience on writers like Thomas Mann, Broch, Brecht, Feuchtwanger and many others is only just beginning to be investigated.

'Influence', as often as not, implies 'impulsion' rather than 'imitation'; a point forcibly made by Ludwig Tieck when he spoke of the relation of his Bluebeard comedy *Ritter Blaubart* to the work of Carlo Gozzi. 'Without any desire to imitate Gozzi,' Tieck writes, 'I took such pleasure in his fables that I was moved to compose a fantastic tale for the stage in another manner, in a German way.'[25] One is reminded of the maxim enunciated by Leszek Kolakowski in another though related context: 'In cases of philosophical "influence" the active partner is not the one who exerts the influence, but the one on whom the influence is exerted. The reception of the past is not governed by some expansive force immanent in it, but rather by attempts of the present to find, in the past, stimuli which will help it discover the answers to its own present problems.'[26] One need not discount the 'expansive force' of great works of literature, or great philosophical ideas for that matter, to perceive the truth and relevance of Kolakowski's observations.

The analogy suggested by the passage just quoted may serve to remind us that while comparative literary studies deal centrally with the relation of one literature to another, they cannot, and must not, limit their scope to such an extent that they exclude the influence of ideas on literature. In nineteenth-century England, for instance, writers were on the whole affected little by German poetry, drama and

[25] *Dichter über ihre Dichtungen: Ludwig Tieck*, ed. U. Schweikert, Munich 1971, vol. I, p. 112.

[26] Leszek Kolakowski, *Jednostka i nieskończoność*, Warsaw 1958, pp. 611-2.

narrative prose, but very much by German philosophical and aesthetic ideas, filtered through Coleridge, for the most part, or later through Carlyle. Conversely, much of what eighteenth-century German literature received from England was not, itself, purely literary. A recent study of the relation of Herder's thought to Bacon's manages in an exemplary way to demonstrate both the contacts Herder had with Bacon's writings and the affinities independent of direct influence which may be traced in the work of these two very different writers. It concludes:

> Just where [Bacon's] direct influence begins and ends can never be exactly determined. It is sufficient if one can demonstrate that it was indeed real and important, particularly in its effect on the naturalistic side of Herder's thought, although, in a mind so complex and comprehensive as that of Herder, many other sides were necessarily untouched by it. Nonetheless, this influence deserves our attention, because until recently, the naturalistic elements in Herder's thought have too often become obscured by the spiritualistic ones, just as the older Aufklärer and rationalist has been overshadowed by the youthful Stürmer und Dränger or supposed irrationalist, and the student of Bacon and the early Kant by the disciple of Hamann. This distorted perspective can be corrected [. . .] if he is considered not only within the context of the German literary revival, but also within that of European thought at large.[27]

While thus correcting a distorted perspective Nisbet allows, as every investigator must, for genuine parallels and analogies as well as for conscious or unconscious suppression by Herder himself and by his later critics.

André Gide, in a diary-entry for 4 August 1922, has said some memorable things about the way a writer may seek stimulation and confirmation in the work of fellow-writers at home and abroad. I quote, once again, from Justin O'Brien's translation.

> It is not fear of being wrong, it is a need of sympathy that makes me seek with passionate anxiety that stimulus or the recall of my thought in others; that made me [. . .] translate Blake and present my own ethic under cover of Dostoevsky's. If those in whom I recognise my thought had not been there, I doubt whether it would have been much

---

[27] H.B. Nisbet, 'Herder and Francis Bacon', *Modern Language Review* LXII (1967), pp. 282-3.

hampered — but its expression would perhaps have been different. It is useless to go back over what has been well said by others. — Nothing is so absurd as that accusation of *influence* (in which certain critics excel every time they note a resemblance). — How many things, on the contrary, I *have not said* because I later discovered them in others! Nietzsche's influence on me? [...] I was already writing *L'Immoraliste* when I discovered him. Who could say how much he got in my way [...] ? And how my book was shorn of all I disliked to *repeat*.[28]

Two things especially are of note here. One is the phrase about presenting 'my own ethic under cover of Dostoevsky's': what interests us most in Gide's comments on Dostoevsky, or Broch's on Joyce, is the light these shed on Gide's, or Broch's, own ideas, ideals and literary practices. The second is more important still: the notion that 'influence' may be a matter of *suppression*, causing an artist to keep back ideas he had worked out for himself but then found perfectly formulated elsewhere. One might term this 'negative influence' — a description more usually reserved for reaction against older works of literature and ideas, for rejection and conscious parodying. Elias Canetti has recently speculated whether one could construct the biography of a man by taking into account everything that repelled him, everything he felt driven to react against. 'Instead of a literary history of influences it would be more instructive to write a history of counter-influences. Counter-images, not always obvious on the surface, are more important than models.'[29] A Russian critic, A.L. Bem, had in fact suggested as early as 1927 that the concept 'influence by repulsion' might usefully be added to our critical armoury.[30]

Gide and Canetti may make us more cautious and subtle in our approach to the history of ideas — they cannot, however, shake our faith in the value of studies like those of Lovejoy, Tillyard or Paul Hazard, or weaken the arguments with which Anthony Thorlby defends the stress that comparative literature students in the University of Sussex are encouraged to place on the history of ideas. 'Literature,' Thorlby has written,

[28] *Journals, 1889-1949*, Harmondsworth 1967, pp. 352-3.

[29] Elias Canetti, 'Aufzeichnungen 1969', *Jahresring 71-72*, Stuttgart 1971, p. 13.

[30] Quoted by Donald Fanger, *Dostoevsky and Romantic Realism*, ed. cit., p. 252.

speaks to us immediately about things other than beauty: about religious and social attitudes, about moral and emotional values; and not about these things in the abstract, but about what they feel like in practice, in the experience of people. It is the variety of this experience on subjects like fear and freedom and forgiveness which may in the end form the basis of comparative studies, in conjunction with non-literary materials bearing on the same questions, as they have been understood by philosophers, say, or sociologists, psychologists, historians [. . .] Precisely *this* kind of comparison is capable of throwing into high relief what is distinctive in literature: which is certainly not that it is remote from truth, but rather that it makes other statements of truth seem remote from experience.[31]

The analysis of the different ways in which the subjects of Kant's concern, for instance, are re-experienced and modified in the work of Schiller and Kleist on the one hand and that of Sartre on the other, may as legitimately form part of comparative literary studies as the manner in which writers all over sixteenth- and seventeenth-century Europe used the concept of a Great Chain of Being, or the varieties of eighteenth-century 'Enlightenment' represented by the work of Voltaire and that of Lessing.

Another kind of 'influence' study relates closely to 'fortune' or 'reception' studies: the investigation of the different *aspects* of a given writer that appeal to writers in another language and appear in their work. An instructive case is that of James Fenimore Cooper, whose *Leather-stocking* tales were eagerly read all over Europe in the nineteenth century. For the Austrian novelist Adalbert Stifter these provided models of nature-description and of the integration of figures into a certain kind of landscape; to Balzac they offered rather a view of struggles between irreconcilable interests which matched a view he had himself come to take in a very different setting. Cooper's novels provided, for Balzac, a repertoire of images and analogies which he could use in his effort to evoke something very far removed from Cooper's wilderness: the spirit of nineteenth-century Paris. Harry Levin, in *The Gates of Horn* (1963) has some excellent pages on the later Balzac's use of Cooper:

---

[31] *The Times Literary Supplement*, 25 July 1968, p. 794; and *Yearbook of Comparative and General Literature* XVII (1968), p. 81.

Writing shortly before the socialist revolution of 1848, Balzac refers the question of property back to the land itself and to man's primitive warfare over possession. One need not travel to America, remarks the journalist Etienne Blondet, in order to behold Cooper's redskins. 'After all, it's an Indian's life surrounded by enemies, and I am defending my scalp,' announces Vautrin, when he makes his appearance on the stage. 'Paris, you see, is like a forest in the new world, agitated by twenty sorts of savage tribes — Illinois and Hurons living on the products of the different social classes,' so he warns Rastignac in *Le Père Goriot*. 'You are hunting after millions.' His own role is not so much the diabolical tempter as the frontier guide, who teaches younger men to bait their traps and track their prey, and who blazes a trail through the pathless faubourgs. It is ironic that Cooper should have been living in Paris during these very years, trying to recapture the earlier spirit of Natty Bumppo in *The Deerslayer* and *The Pathfinder*. Meanwhile Balzac had been pursuing his own particular tribe of savages — *mohicans en spencer et hurons en redingote*, as they were designated by André Le Breton [. . .] Cooper had come along to provide epic comparisons for the bourgeoisie and to point, where civilization breaks down, to the harsher backgrounds of nature. It is the stark antagonism, the brute ferocity, the endless hostilities, so near to the innocuous surfaces of the *Leather-stocking* novels, that account for their continued influence over the *Comédie humaine*. The poor relation, Lisbeth Fischer, is the Mohican in ambush [. . .][32]

This more indirect presence of Cooper's world in Balzac's mature novels is more interesting and rewarding than any direct imitation: Harry Levin rightly devotes little space to the younger Balzac's endeavour to model *Le Dernier Chouan* on *The Last of the Mohicans*.

In an important 'Note on Influences and Conventions',[33] Claudio Guillén introduces a different distinction, between 'direct' and 'indirect' influence, by asking the question: 'Did a Renaissance poet have to read Petrarch in order to write a Petrarchan sonnet?' The answer, of course, is 'No'; but this does not invalidate the indirect influence of Petrarch, working through a set of literary conventions which Guillén terms 'collective, shared influences'. J.T. Shaw, in an essay on Lermontov and Byron, takes up and elaborates Guillén's distinction.[34] Lermontov, Shaw demonstrates, took over

[32] Harry Levin, *The Gates of Horn*, Galaxy ed., New York 1966, pp. 211-2.

[33] *Literature as System: Essays toward the Theory of Literature*, Princeton 1971, p. 61.

[34] In *Comparative Literature — Method and Perspective*, ed. N.P. Stallknecht and N. Frenz, Southern Illinois U.P., 1961.

from Pushkin the model of the Byronic tales in verse; but he also went to Byron direct, adopting features Pushkin had not introduced into his own Byron-inspired tales. 'An author,' Shaw concludes, 'may introduce the influence of a foreign author into a literary tradition, and then, as in the case of the Byronic tradition in Russia, it may proceed largely from the influence of the native author (i.e. Pushkin). But as the tradition continues, it may be enriched by another native author [who goes] back to the foreign author for materials or tonalities or images or effects which were not adopted by the first author.'[3][5] Writers do learn from each other, even across linguistic frontiers, and few questions interest the literary historian more than *what* they learn, and how they apply the lesson.

Another way of reacting to literary stimuli from outside has been called, by Anna Balakian, 'negative influence': a not altogether happy term for a revolt against works whose popularity is thought to be leading native literature into a wrong direction. One may think here of the rejection of some French seventeenth- and eighteenth-century drama by German writers from Lessing to A.W. Schlegel; or of Wordsworth's attack, in the Preface to *Lyrical Ballads*, on the 'frantic novels and sickly and stupid [. . .] tragedies' with which translators from the German are said to satisfy his contemporaries' 'degrading thirst after outrageous stimulation'. Wordsworth sees his *Lyrical Ballads* as 'a feeble effort to counteract' this thirst; and in assessing the influence of German on English writings in the Romantic period, one must take cognisance of such 'negative influence', such stimulus to rejection and counter-effort. Tieck's disappointment by Webster's *The White Devil* played as decisive a part in the composition of his novel *Vittoria Accorombona* as Shaw's dislike of the way Shakespeare and Schiller handled the Joan of Arc story played in the composition of *St. Joan.*

Positive and negative stimuli may, in fact, work together in the same period and even in the same person. Leonard Forster has convincingly shown, in *The Icy Fire*, how the imagery and *topoi* of European Petrarchism could be used by

[35] op. cit., p. 68.

Shakespeare with entire seriousness in one sonnet only to be denied and parodied in the next (in Sonnet 130, for instance, which begins with the line 'My mistress' eyes are nothing like the sun'). 'What for Petrarch himself was deadly serious became for his successors a game, which like all games can be serious or not, as circumstances require [. . .] It would be as serious or as frivolous as you wanted. It was surely this flexibility which accounted for its enormous popularity for so long.'[36] And again: 'Anti-Petrarchism is only an aspect of Petrarchism'.[37] This co-presence of Petrarchism and anti-Petrarchism remained a feature of European literature until well into the nineteenth century; Baudelaire's *Une Charogne* makes its most powerful effects, as Sainte-Beuve was the first to notice, by using Petrarchan imagery and *topoi* in the description of a decaying carcase. Here 'influence' study merges with that of literary allusion, quotation, stylization and parody.

Trahison créatrice also belongs into this context. A work may flourish in a social and literary context for which it was never intended: Robert Escarpit, in, an essay entitled ' "Creative Treason" as a Key to Literature'[38] has cited the example of *Gulliver's Travels*, a bitter satire on political, academic and religious abuses in the eighteenth century, a classic of adult misanthropy, which now lives on in various French and German adaptations as a thrilling tale for French and German children.[39] A different instance is supplied by Anna Balakian's study of *The Literary Origins of French Surrealism*,[40] where we can watch André Breton's imagination fired by the *mistranslation* of a passage from the works of Achim von Arnim. It was precisely this (unrecognised) mistranslation, Anna Balakian assures us, which

[36] Forster, *The Icy Fire: Five Studies in European Petrarchism*, Cambridge 1969, pp. 66-7.

[37] ibid., p. 57.

[38] Robert Escarpit, ' "Creative Treason" as a key to literature', *Yearbook of Comparative and General Literature* X (1961), p. 20.

[39] There are signs that the same process may soon begin to operate on Orwell's *Animal Farm*.

[40] Anna Balakian, *The Literary Origins of French Surrealism*, New York 1947, pp. 37-9.

prompted Breton to raise Arnim even above Hoffmann in the pantheon of surrealists *avant la lettre*. More recent examples would include Ezra Pound's fruitful misunderstanding of the nature of the Chinese ideogram. Such *trahisons créatrices* cannot be called 'influences' in the sense that they materially directed or altered the course of French Surrealism or modern poetry in English: they acted rather as confirmation and encouragement to continue along a path already chosen.

'Influence', J. Brandt Corstius has rightly warned us, must not be confused with 'success':

> The fact that some authors have been, for a longer or shorter period, highly successful outside their own countries does not necessarily imply that they have exerted influence. Researches into such successes may lead to conclusions about literary taste, preferences, fashions, or the power of publicity [...] But success says little or nothing about the literary influence — i.e. about the significance of the successful work of literature, its form and vision, in the country in which this writer from abroad is so [...] popular.[41]

This point is well illustrated by two examples given by Wolfgang Clemen in 'Was ist literarischer Einfluss?'; examples in which 'success' and 'influence' both play a part. The first of these concerns the popularity of Seneca in sixteenth-century England and the many traces that can be found in sixteenth-century drama of Seneca's influence — ranging from the reappearance of whole plots to that of situations and turns of phrase. How comes it, Clemen asks, that Seneca, who wrote closet-dramas never meant for performance, could interest a generation of writers who produced the most theatrically effective plays known to world-literature? Clemen then lists the features of Seneca's work which appealed to the Elizabethans: orotund speeches, moralizing sententiae, delight in rhetorical self-dramatization, a sequence of sensational, terrible happenings. Seneca's influence must not, however, be seen apart from other influences that swelled and modified it: influences from the popular drama of the fourteenth and fifteenth centuries, with its lively stage-action, its movement and bustle, and its closeness to

---

[41] J. Brandt Corstius, *Introduction to the Comparative Study of Literature*, New York 1968, p. 186.

low life. Seneca's influence, Clemen concludes, became effective only because of its conjunction with other influences from mystery and morality plays, interludes and masks, Latin and Italian comedies; all these affected, though none of them can wholly account for, the great flourishing of Elizabethan drama.

The second instructive example I take from Clemen is the European success of Macpherson's *Ossian*. What happened here, clearly, is that the age sought for a legitimation, in the past, of some of its own ideals and literary practices. Macpherson responded to this by projecting sentiments and forms of his own time into the past, giving them the patina of ancient Scottish poetry, and then presenting the whole as an ancient epic. In emulating this supposed ancient epic, in allowing its rhythms, its sentiments, its images, to affect their own work, Goethe, Herder and others were giving what they supposed to be a historical legitimation to tendencies of their own time — tendencies they had themselves helped to shape and direct. The eighteenth century, Clemen concludes, had here itself created the influence from the past to which it consented to submit.

The study of 'influence' has often been pursued in a mechanical, unimaginative way that deserves all the strictures it has attracted; but Guillén, Clemen and Anna Balakian are surely right in vindicating its function in comparative literary study. Three caveats, however, pronounced by scholars who have themselves made important contributions to this field of investigation, deserve to be heard and heeded. The first comes from Irene Samuel's *Plato and Milton*:

In order to appraise the influence of one writer on another, we must start, of course, from explicit references. But we need not take a narrow view of the transmission of thought from mind to mind. Only a pedant would lift word after word from another's page, or retain in separate compartments of his mind what he has learned from this source and what from that. A thought once assimilated will readily flow into channels far from its original source. Thus, if Milton truly accepts some definite view from Plato, he is not likely to tag it at every use, much less to name the dialogue or epistle in which he found it. In large part the effect of a writer upon any reader cannot be traced back to isolated passages; the spirit of the whole is more likely to remain with him than a series of excerpts.[42]

The second caveat comes from Henry Gifford, who insists that the most rewarding comparisons

are those that writers themselves have accepted or challenged their readers to make — those that spring from 'the shock of recognition', where one writer has become conscious that an affinity exists between another and himself. Henry James felt this about Turgenev, Pound felt it about Propertius, Pushkin about Byron.[43]

And last but not least there is Anna Balakian's timely warning against over-emphasising the role of influence:

One is sometimes led to wonder whether any study of influence is truly justified unless it succeeds in elucidating the particular qualities of the borrower, in revealing along with the influence, and almost in spite of it, what is infinitely more important: the turning-point at which the writer frees himself of the influence and finds his originality.[44]

No comparatist can afford to ignore the delicate balance, the dialectical relationship, of influence and originality, convention and innovation, conscious learning and spontaneous or deliberate transmutation.

---

[42] Irene Samuel, *Plato and Milton*, Ithaca 1965, p.3.

[43] *Comparative Literature*, London 1969, p. 73.

[44] 'Influence and Literary Fortune', *Yearbook of Comparative and General Literature* XI (1962), p. 29.

5.

Translation and Adaptation

Translation has been called, by Wilhelm von Humboldt,

> one of the labours most essential to any literature; partly because it introduces those ignorant of foreign languages to forms of art and humanity which otherwise they would never come to know — and this is an important gain for any nation; but partly also, and especially, because it widens the capacity for meaning and expression possessed by one's own language.[1]

It provides the most important channel through which international influences can flow; its investigation is therefore of the greatest importance to the comparatist. Two main sources have been distinguished for modern European translation. The first of these is the endeavour to translate the Bible, an endeavour which demanded highest respect before the word of God and the highest degree of selfless devotion on the part of the translator, for whom it would have been blasphemy to seek self-expression through his version of words that enshrined eternal truth. The translator had to mediate between the revelation contained in the Bible and those of his fellow-countrymen who could not understand the original Hebrew and Greek: a mediation which required concern over idiom and equivalence (as demonstrated in Luther's *Epistle on Translation* [*Sendbrief von Dolmetschen*] for instance) only in so far as the pure truth of God's word could not be effectively communicated in literal translation. The other source is of course translation from the ancient authors, in which every age could mirror itself and with which poets have tried in every generation — especially

---

[1] cf. *Wilhelm von Humboldts Gesammelte Werke* (Akademie-Ausgabe), Berlin 1905-1920, vol. VIII, p. 130.

before the onset of Romantic historicism — to mingle their own spirit and that of their time. The Authorized Version keeps closer to the original text than Chapman's, or Pope's, Homer.

There is, in practice, no absolute distinction between the two modes represented by translation from the Bible and translation from the Classics — they represent 'ideal types' of two approaches described by Goethe and Schleiermacher, who were both, it should be noted, adept translators. 'There are,' said Goethe in his eulogy of Wieland, 'two maxims for translators; one demands that the author belonging to some other nation should be brought over to us, so that we can regard him as our own; the other demands of us that we should go across to the stranger and accustom ourselves to his circumstances, his manner of speaking, his peculiarities'; a formulation which is strikingly similar to a better-known, later pronouncement by Friedrich Schleiermacher: 'A translator either leaves the author as much alone as is possible and moves the reader towards him; or he leaves the reader as much alone as is possible and moves the author towards him.'[2] The first method, taken to its extreme, leads to J.L. Borges's famous image of the man who laboriously translates *Don Quixote* into identical Spanish; the only *traduttore* who cannot be called *traditore* is the one who reproduces his original exactly, word for word. The second extreme leads to Goethe's *West-Eastern Divan*, where a poem like *Ecstasy and Desire* [*Selige Sehnsucht*] takes off from one by Hafiz but departs so radically from the metre and spirit of the original that a Persian reader familiar with Hafiz's work would hardly realize what that original was — unless he were alerted by the knowledge that Goethe's poem bore, at one time, a title which specifically referred to a ghazal by Hafiz: *Buch Sad, Gasele 1.*

An account of the value of translation studies for students of Comparative Literature may begin with a glance at a well-known example: Hamlet's 'To be or not to be' monologue as translated by Voltaire and by A.W. Schlegel.

---

[2] cf. A. Huyssen, *Die frühromantische Konzeption von Übersetzung und Aneignung*, Zürich 1969, pp. 18, 51, 188.

Hamlet. To be, or not to be, that is the question,
Whether 'tis nobler in the mind to suffer
The slings and arrows of outrageous fortune,
Or to take arms against a sea of troubles,
5   And by opposing, end them. To die, to sleep —
No more, and by a sleep to say we end
The heart-ache, and the thousand natural shocks
That flesh is heir to; 'tis a consummation
Devoutly to be wished to die to sleep!
10 To sleep, perchance to dream, ay there's the rub,
For in that sleep of death what dreams may come
When we have shuffled off this mortal coil
Must give us pause — there's the respect
That makes calamity of so long life:
15 For who would bear the whips and scorns of time,
The oppressor's wrong, the proud man's contumely,
The pangs of disprized love, the law's delay,
The insolence of office, and the spurns
That patient merit of th'unworthy takes,
20 When he himself might his quietus make
With a bare bodkin; who would fardels bear,
To grunt and sweat under a weary life,
But that the dread of something after death,
The undiscovered country, from whose bourn
25 No traveller returns, puzzles the will,
And makes us rather bear those ills we have,
Than fly to others that we know not of?
Thus conscience does make cowards of us all,
And thus the native hue of resolution
30 Is sicklied o'er with the pale cast of thought,
And enterprises of great pitch and moment
With this regard their currents turn awry,
And lose the name of action.

                                        Hamlet, Act III, Scene 1
                                        (Dover Wilson's text)

Demeure; it faut choisir, et passer à l'instant
De la vie à la mort, ou de l'être au néant.
Dieux cruels! s'il en est, éclairez mon courage.
Faut-il vieillir courbé sous la main qui m'outrage,
5   Supporter ou finir mon malheur et mon sort?
Qui suis-je? qui m'arrête? et qu'est-ce que la mort?
C'est la fin de nos maux, c'est mon unique asile;
Après de longs transports, c'est un sommeil tranquille;
On s'endort, et tout meurt. Mais un affreux réveil
10 Doit succéder peut-être aux douceurs du sommeil.
On nous menace, on dit que cette courte vie
De tourments éternels est aussitôt suivie.

O mort! moment fatal! affreuse éternité!
Tout coeur à ton seul nom se glace épouvanté.
15 Eh! qui pourrait sans toi supporter cette vie,
De nos prêtres menteurs bénir l'hypocrisie,
D'une indigne maîtresse encenser les erreurs,
Ramper sous un ministre, adorer ses hauteurs,
Et montrer les langueurs de son âme abattue
20 A des amis ingrats qui détournent la vue?
La mort serait trop douce en ces extrémités;
Mais le scrupule parle, et nous crie: Arrêtez.
Il défend à nos mains cet heureux homicide,
Et d'un héros guerrier fait un chrétien timide, *etc.*

Voltaire: 'Sur la Tragédie',
Lettres sur les Anglais, 1734

Voltaire himself comments on this translation, in *Lettres sur
les Anglais*, as follows:

Do not believe that I have here rendered the English word for word;
woe to the literal translators who, translating every word, enervate the
sense! Here it may indeed be said that the letter killeth, but the spirit
giveth life.

What Voltaire has done is to transpose Shakespeare into French
classical verse, substituting alexandrines for iambic pentameter
and polite diction for Shakespearean vigour. In lines 16 to 20
he has gone further: the 'lying preachers' and 'unworthy
mistress', 'prêtres menteurs' and 'indigne maîtresse', are pure
Voltaire; nor is Prince Hamlet likely to crawl to a minister
and adore his pretensions:

Ramper sous un ministre, adorer ses hauteurs.

Voltaire feels quite free to take side-swipes at his own
enemies and transform Hamlet's speech into a platform from
which to air his own prejudices.

With A.W. Schlegel's German version of the same speech,
published some seventy years later, we enter a different world:
an attempt to come as close as possible to Shakespeare's
meaning, imagery and rhythm.

Seyn oder Nichtseyn, das ist hier die Frage:
Ob's edler im Gemüth, die Pfeil' und Schleudern
Des wüthenden Geschicks erdulden, oder

Sich waffnend gegen eine See von Plagen,
5   Durch Widerstand sie enden. Sterben — schlafen —
Nichts weiter! und zu wissen, dass ein Schlaf
Das Herzweh und die tausend Stösse endet,
Die unsers Fleisches Erbtheil — 's ist ein Ziel
Aufs innigste zu wünschen. Sterben — schlafen —
10   Schlafen! Vielleicht auch träumen! — Ja, da liegt's:
Was in dem Schlaf für Träume kommen mögen,
Wenn wir den Drang des Ird'schen abgeschüttelt,
Das zwingt uns still zu stehn. Das ist die Rücksicht,
Die Elend lässt zu hohen Jahren kommen.
15   Denn wer ertrüg' der Zeiten Spott und Geissel,
Des Mächt'gen Druck, des Stolzen Misshandlungen,
Verschmähter Liebe Pein, des Rechtes Aufschub,
Den Übermuth der Ämter, und die Schmach,
Die Unwerth schweigendem Verdienst erweist,
20   Wenn er sich selbst in Ruhstand setzen könnte
Mit einer Nadel bloss? Wer trüge Lasten,
Und stöhnt' und schwitzte unter Lebensmüh'?
Nur dass die Furcht vor etwas nach dem Tod —
Das unentdeckte Land, von dess Bezirk
25   Kein Wandrer wiederkehrt — den Willen irrt,
Dass wir die Übel, die wir haben, lieber
Ertragen, als zu unbekannten fliehn.
So macht Gewissen Feige aus uns allen;
Der angebohrnen Farbe der Entschliessung
30   Wird des Gedankens Blässe angekränkelt;
Und Unternehmungen voll Mark und Nachdruck,
Durch diese Rücksicht aus der Bahn gelenkt,
Verlieren so der Handlung Nahmen.

Here too Margaret Atkinson and other commentators have
pointed to important differences, aspects of Shakespeare
which even a great translator like Schlegel could not convey
into German. In the German version the images do not crowd
as thick and fast as in the English; the verse-movement is less
springy and energetic, with more lines ending on an unac-
cented syllable; the expressive alliterative emphasis of such
lines as 'Thus conscience does make cowards of us all' is lost;
and in German it proved impossible to match the original's
juxtaposition of stately words originating in Latin with more
homely ones deriving from Anglo-Saxon. ''tis a consum-
mation/Devoutly to be wished' is more powerful and
impressive than ''s ist ein Ziel/Aufs innigste zu wünschen' —
though here one must also remember that Schlegel deliber-

ately avoided archaising, that he chose, rightly, to translate Shakespeare's seventeenth-century English into nineteenth-century German. As a whole, however, Schlegel's Shakespeare translations are a magnificent achievement in Schleiermacher's first mode — that of bringing the reader to the author, of reproducing the author's manner and matter, *Stoff, Gehalt* and *Form*, as far as ever possible in the language of the translator's time and place. The contrast with the mode represented by Voltaire is absolute.

English readers will be inclined to see in Schlegel's versions of Shakespeare a supreme example of that middle way, the way of 'paraphrase', which Dryden advocated in his celebrated discussion of the translator's art.

All translation, I suppose, may be reduced to these three heads.

First, that of metaphrase, or turning an author word by word, and line by line, from one language into another. Thus, or near in this manner, was Horace his *Art of Poetry* translated by Ben Jonson. The second way is that of paraphrase, or translation with latitude, where the author is kept in view by the translator, so as never to be lost, but his words are not so strictly followed as his sense; and that too is admitted to be amplified, but not altered. Such is Mr. Waller's translation of Virgil's Fourth *Aeneid*. The third way is that of imitation, where the translator (if now he has not lost that name) assumes the liberty not only to vary from the words and sense, but to forsake them both as he sees occasion; and taking only some general hints from the original, to run division on the groundwork, as he pleases. Such is Mr. Cowley's practice in turning two Odes of Pindar, and one of Horace, into English.[3]

What is astonishing, however, is the extent to which Schlegel succeeded in adhering to the sequence of Shakespeare's words as well to his sense; avoiding amplification as well as alteration; making most previous translations seem, by contrast, exercises in imitation or metaphrase.

Schlegel's work is not exempt, of course, from the rule recently enunciated by Henry Gifford: 'The first law of translation is clear: nothing can be taken as final.'[4] The converse rule, however, applies no less: the great translations of the past never lose their authority and their appeal

[3] John Dryden, Preface to the *Translations from Ovid's Epistles*, 1680.

[4] *Comparative Literature*, London 1969, p. 99.

entirely. The Authorised Version will not, and should not, disappear because of the existence of the New English Bible. Successful contemporary or near-contemporary translations will always retain a special importance. To read Rabelais in Urquhart's version or in Fischart's, to read Cervantes and Matteo Alemán in the translation by James Mabbe, is still a powerful and worth-while experience; more powerful and more worth-while if we are able to appreciate what features of their original the older translators have been able to reproduce, what they have lost, and what they have added.

It is not [. . .] a merely antiquarian preference which finds in these Elizabethan translations the perfect expression, in English, of the stories of the Spanish 'Golden Century'. That century was one in which literature was still something to be read aloud, something in which the sound had a value as well as the sense; and the translators had to find a means of giving English readers an echo of the 'resounding grace' of the Castilian tongue, as well as a reply to its home thrusts and compressed, proverbial phrases. They were, perhaps, more successful with the former than with the latter; for when their versions are compared with the originals, it will generally be found that it is not in the fine phrases and courtly circumlocutions that the translators are beaten, but in the directness of the thrust which goes right home. Yet the little English words, like the little English ships, could sometimes get round their more powerful opponents, especially when they were handled by such a master as James Mabbe; and in the end, it is not so much the fine phrases which stand out and hold the attention as the conversational turns of expression — things which are as appropriate in modern English as they were then, and which would never occur to any modern purveyor of spurious 'Old English'.[5]

Trend's insistence on the stylistic aspect of the Elizabethan translations he so admires goes with his justified conviction that style is indissolubly connected with thought and substance.

In a study entitled *Seven Agamemnons*, Reuben Brower has tried to demonstrate that translations are, in great measure, created by their public; that the average reader wants to find in a translation the kind of experience which has become identified with 'poetry' in his reading of his own literature, and that the translator who wishes to be read must

---

[5] J.B. Trend, Introduction to *Spanish Short Stories of the Sixteenth Century*, Oxford 1928, pp. v-vi.

in some degree satisfy that want.[6] In support of his thesis Brower analyses a number of English translations of Aeschylus's *Agamemnon*, from the eighteenth to the twentieth centuries, and shows them up as answers given at various times to the question: 'What is poetry?' Brower's demonstration in no way invalidates the view that Voltaire and Schlegel represent not only different ways of responding to this question, but also different degrees of adaptation; the eighteenth-century translator is prone to regard his own society's standards as absolute, while the nineteenth-century translator begins to look more for the *frisson nouveau* which comes from the very 'foreignness' of the translated writer. Herder, who insisted on the uniqueness of each culture and the need to appreciate that uniqueness, had not written in vain.

The post-Herderian, post-Schlegelian feeling is clearly expressed in Rolfe Humphries' essay on translating from Latin into English verse: 'A good translation [. . .] ought, for the sake of the contemporary reader, to sound, on the whole, more familiar than strange; yet in justice to the original some hint at least of his quality, some soupçon of his foreign accent, must be kept.'[7] The growing volume of complaints about Scott Moncrieff's justly celebrated translation from Proust would have seemed ridiculous to Voltaire but just to Schlegel. The transmutation of the title *A la recherche du temps perdu* into *Remembrance of Things Past* may awake pleasing reminiscences in readers who know Shakespeare's sonnets; but does it not, through that very fact, summon up inappropriate associations? Where, Harry Levin has asked, is the sense of searching and experimenting present in *recherche*, where that of *wasted* as well as *lost* time in *temps perdu*? *Within a Budding Grove* may answer very well the expectations a reader brought up on Georgian poetry has of a 'poetic' title: but where are the girls, where is the shade, of *A l'ombre des jeunes filles en fleurs*? And does not *The Sweet Cheat Gone* (for *Albertine disparue*) respond too literally to the expectations of readers of Walter de le Mare? Does it not import into Proust suggestions which have no place there,

---

[6] *On Translation*, ed. R. Brower, Galaxy ed., New York 1966, pp. 173-95.

[7] Brower, op. cit., p. 60.

whether these derive from a recollection of the original context of that phrase or not?

The trouble with translations, it has often been said, is that they can be properly judged only by those who have no need of them. 'To test the closeness of any translation to its original,' David Lodge has recently told us, 'one would have to be not only bi-lingual but — to coin an ugly phrase — bicultural, i.e. possessed of the whole complex of emotions, associations, and ideas which intricately relate a nation's language to its life and tradition, but possessed not only of one such complex — as we all are to some extent — but of two.'[8] This describes, accurately, the all-but-impossible ideal comparatists set themselves to accomplish; and it suggests a reason why the scrutiny of translation has come to loom large in comparative literature courses offered by universities. Studies in the theory and history of translation are increasingly being supplemented by practice in the craft of literary translation as well as analysis of selected renderings by different translators at different times. This is a welcome development; for comparatists are uniquely qualified to perform the important task of investigating the nature and accuracy of existing translations and that of gauging the degree of distortion introduced into literary criticism and literary theory by the use of such translations. Recent correspondence in the *Times Literary Supplement* has made it clear, for instance, that there is room for a close examination of differences between the novels of Günter Grass in their German and in their English version — a task already performed for Swedish translations of Grass by research students at Stockholm University. A comparative study of Milton and Plato revealed, in 1947, a serious error in the Columbia edition of Milton, where the Latin sentence

Hoc argumento Plato miseras civitates auguratur, quae medicorum et judicum multitudine indigent, quia multum quoque et intemperantiam et injustitiam in ea civitate versari necesse est

is translated:

---

[8] *Language of Fiction: Essays in Criticism and Verbal Analysis of the English Novel*, London 1966, p. 20.

By means of this argument Plato conjectures that 'those states are wretched which lack a multitude of physicians and judges, since necessarily much intemperance and injustice will be practised in such a state'.

Clearly, as Irene Samuel points out in *Plato and Milton*,[9] a reference to Plato's *Republic* 3, 405 will show that Plato said the very opposite, and that Milton's 'multitudine indigeant' must therefore mean '*need* a multitude'. One is reminded of what Bernard Shaw had to say, in the preface to the first edition of *The Perfect Wagnerite*, about the importance of submitting oneself to the *ideas* of the author whose work is being rendered into another language: 'The earlier attempts to translate [Wagner's] numerous pamphlets and essays into English resulted in ludicrous mixtures of pure nonsense with the absurdest distortions of his ideas into the ideas of his translators. We now have a translation which is a masterpiece of interpretation and an eminent addition to our literature; but that is not because its author, Mr. Ashton Ellis, knows the German dictionary better than his predecessors. He is simply in possession of Wagner's ideas, which were to them inconceivable'.[10]

Scrutiny of other texts may range from the detection of the mistranslation from Arnim which induced Breton, according to Anna Balakian, to admire that writer as a forerunner of Surrealism,[11] to that of the occasional

[9] Irene Samuel, *Plato and Milton*, Cornell University Press, 1965 ed., p. 24.

[10] Bernard Shaw, *Major Critical Essays*, London 1932, p. 165.

[11] In his Preface to the 1933 edition of the translation of Arnim's tales by Théophile Gautier *fils*, Breton quotes, with approval, from Arnim's *Die Majoratsherren*: 'Je discerne avec peine ce que je vois avec les yeux de la réalité de ce que voit mon imagination' ['I find it hard to distinguish what I see with the eyes of reality from that which my imagination sees']. What Arnim in fact wrote was: 'Ich kann genau unterscheiden was ich mit dem Auge der Wahrheit sehen muss oder was ich mir gestalte' ['I can distinguish *precisely* what I must see with the eye of truth from that which I shape for myself']. Anna Balakian comments: 'He [i.e. Arnim] can *exactly* distinguish the difference and sees to it that the reader does the same; the basis of his representation of the unusual is not a voluntary disorder of the mental process. It would appear that André Breton faithfully adhered to the mistranslation of Gautier, which made Arnim's text much more interesting from the point of view of Surrealism than the original. Had he consulted Arnim instead of trusting Gautier for his citation he would undoubtedly have lost a good argument — and perhaps an ancestor!' (Anna Balakian, *The Literary Origins of Surrealism: A New Mysticism in French Poetry*, New York 1947, pp. 38-9).

uncertainty which creeps even into Harry Levin's pronouncements when he feels moved to quote German rather than
French or English material: as in *The Gates of Horn*, where
Goethe is said to have defined the novel to Eckermann as 'the
occurrence of an unprecedented event'. What Goethe said in
effect ('. . . was ist eine Novelle anders als eine sich ereignete
unerhörte Begebenheit') clearly refers to the *Novelle*, a
short-story form, and not to the novel.

Such occasional slips do not lessen the respect every
comparatist must feel for Harry Levin's important contribution to our discipline; we will certainly not find Levin
prepared to build elaborate hypotheses on the evidence of a
translation alone. This is the trap into which Erich Fromm
falls in his widely-read *The Forgotten Language*, where the
opening of Kafka's *The Trial* is quoted from the standard
English version by Willa and Edwin Muir: 'Someone must
have been telling lies about Joseph K., for without having
done anything wrong he was arrested one fine morning.'
Fromm then goes on to comment as follows:

What does 'arrested' mean? It is an interesting word which has a double
meaning. To be arrested can mean to be taken into custody by police
officers and to be arrested can mean to be stopped in one's growth and
development. An accused man is 'arrested' by the police, and an
organism is 'arrested' in its normal development. The manifest story
uses 'arrested' in the former sense. Its symbolic meaning, however, is to
be understood in the latter. K. has an awareness that he is arrested and
blocked in his own development.[12]

A glance at the German original will show that what Kafka in
fact wrote was *verhaftet*, a word which does *not* mean
'stopped in one's growth and development'.

Comparative literary studies may concern themselves also
with the impact of translations, and the activity of translating, on the work of given writers or on literary movements.
It is surely significant that Dostoevsky began his literary
career with a translation of Balzac's *Eugénie Grandet*; and
that Sir Walter Scott's very first publication resulted,
indirectly, from the enthusiasm provoked in Edinburgh by
Laetitia Aikin's reading, in 1793 and 1794, of an English

[12] Erich Fromm, op. cit., New York 1957, p. 250.

version of Bürger's ballad *Lenore*. In his *Essay on Imitations of the Ancient Ballad* (1830), Scott tells of his efforts to procure a copy of the original; of his attempt to translate it and another ballad by Bürger (*Der wilde Jäger*); of his issuing the two translations together in a thin quarto published by Manners and Miller; and of his delighted discovery that popular Scottish and popular German poetry had much in common.

It requires only a smattering of both languages, to see at what cheap expense, even of vocables and rhymes, the popular poetry of the one may be transferred to the other. Hardly any thing is more flattering to a Scottish student of German; it resembles the unexpected discovery of an old friend in a foreign land.

And so it was a natural step, for Scott, to pass from translation to imitation: 'by degrees', he tells us, 'I acquired sufficient confidence to attempt the imitation of what I admired.'[13] The first result of this newly found confidence was the ballad *Glenfilas*, which was followed by another ballad in the same manner, *The Eve of St. John*. When Germans later received Scott's works with general acclamation, they were thus acclaiming something to which they had themselves given an initial impetus.

The relationship of Brecht to Arthur Waley is an even more instructive case. Patrick Bridgwater has unravelled it in an excellent article, which shows that right from the start Brecht's style as a lyric poet had some of the austere beauty and grace we associate with Far Eastern poetry; that he lost this at the time of his political conversion, which tempted him to interminable hack verse; but that he was helped to recover the concentration and grace of his early verse by his study of Waley's English translations from the Chinese and Japanese.[14] In his *Chinese Poems* [*Chinesische Gedichte*] of 1938, and again in 1950, Brecht acknowledged his debt by retranslating some of Waley's versions into German.

Translations play an important part, not only in the

[13] 'Essay on Imitations of the Ancient Ballad' written in 1830 and prefixed to Scott's *Minstrelsy of the Scottish Border*, part III.

[14] P. Bridgwater, 'Arthur Waley and Brecht', *German Life and Letters* XVII, 1964.

development of individual writers, but also in that of literary movements and genres. How central was the role of translation and its theory in the German Romantic movement, for instance! 'Except for the Romans', Novalis wrote to A.W. Schlegel in 1797, 'we are the only nation which has felt so imperiously the urge to translate and which owes to this urge so much of its education. This accounts for many similarities between our literary culture and that of the later Romans. This urge is an indication of the exalted and original character of the German people. To be German means to be at once cosmopolitan and extremely original. Only for us have translations signified enlargement. It requires a high degree of poetic morality, sacrifice of one's inclinations, to submit oneself to true translation. One translates because of genuine love of the beautiful and of one's own country's literature. Translating is as good as writing new poetic works — only it is more difficult, depends on a rarer gift.' And Novalis adds, in words which reveal something of the analogical force the German Romantics felt in the activity of translating: 'In the end *all* poetry is translation.'[15]

Those who study literary genres and sub-genres will also have to take the history of translation into account; will have to study the *belles infidèles*, versions which by their very beauty betray their original (how much more satisfying the poetry of Edgar Allan Poe is in French than it is in English!), and versions which owe their obvious departure from literal faithfulness to a shift in taste and sensibility. A.A. Parker, in his study of the picaresque novel,[16] has provided some particularly instructive examples of *trahison créatrice*. Lesage's 1732 translation of *Guzmán de Alfarache*

reduces the novel to the bare bones of the narrative by omitting not only the 'moralities' but all references to religious teaching as well. Furthermore, Lesage makes Guzmán at the very end denounce the conspiracy of the galley-slaves, not in order to make right and justice prevail as is the case in Alemán, but in order to seek revenge on the companion who had falsely accused him of stealing. For Lesage, Guzmán is a cynical cad to the very end.[17]

[15] Letter to A.W. Schlegel dated 30 November 1797 (Novalis, *Briefe und Dokumente*, ed. E. Wasmuth, Heidelberg 1954, pp. 367-8).

[16] A.A. Parker, *Literature and the Delinquent: The Picaresque Novel in Spain and Europe 1599-1753*, Edinburgh 1967.

[17] ibid., p. 116.

An even more radical transformation, along similar lines, may be found in La Geneste's translation of Quevedo's *Life and Adventures of Don Pablos the Sharper* [*El buscón*], revised by Raclots in 1699. Parker seeks one reason for such changes in the stricter separation of styles imposed by French neo-classicism, in the re-establishment of a barrier between the comic and the serious which the earlier Spanish writers had in part removed: 'Because *Guzmán de Alfarache* was realistic it could not be serious; its moral and religious interests had therefore eventually to be eliminated. Because *El buscón* was comic it had to have a happy ending; all that made its delinquent protagonist undeserving of success and prosperity had therefore to be eliminated'.[18] These translations, Parker demonstrates, show up clearly a turning-point in the history of the picaresque novel in Europe:

In passing from Alemán, Quevedo and Grimmelshausen to Lesage, *via* the French translations, the literature of delinquency has in fact turned a somersault. The reform of Gil Blas, and the optimistic 'disenchant-ment' that motivates his withdrawal to the prosperous life of a country gentleman, would have aroused in all three a sardonic laughter. The only optimism Grimmelshausen could feel lay in the possibility of eremitical solitude away from the warfare of human life. The only optimism Alemán could feel was belief in divine grace; if this is an illusion, he would have said, then there are no grounds for hoping that the delinquent can ever cease to be. As regards Quevedo, the question of optimism or pessimism is altogether too crude for the level on which he presents delinquency — that of the suffering endured by a man who is an outsider, because of a burden of shame and guilt too heavy to be borne without resentment or revenge.[19]

One need not regard the early picaresque novel quite as solemnly as Professor Parker to agree that in turning from *El buscón* and *Simplicissimus* to *Gil Blas* and *Colonel Jack* we pass to something much less tense and much less fraught with tragic possibilities. A study of translations by Lesage and La Geneste can help us define a transformation whose cause must be sought in the history of Europe and the social history of the nations that compose it as well as in the individual bent, and the individual genius, of the writers that shaped the picaresque tradition.

[18] ibid., p. 120.
[19] ibid., p. 125.

Translation-studies merge readily into 'stylistics'. The special qualities of an author's style, and the literary tradition within which he stands, often become most clearly apparent when one examines the way in which he translates the work of others. Conversely, appreciation of the translated author's style may also be sharpened by seeing what is left out or altered in a congenial translation. 'The inadequacies of a significant translation are creations of insight, critically revealing as no other reading of a poem is. . . . A great poetic translation . . . is criticism in the highest sense. It surrounds the original with a zone of unmastered meaning, an area in which the original declares its own singular life.'[20] A model analysis of this kind has recently been undertaken from one point of view by Hartwig Schulz in a book on rhythmic patterns in modern poetry.[21] Schulz there confronts the first poem of Verlaine's cycle *Sagesse* with its rendering by Stefan George.

Bon chevalier masqué qui chevauche en silence,
Le Malheur a percé mon vieux coeur de sa lance.

Le sang de mon vieux coeur n'a fait qu'un jet vermeil,
Puis s'est évaporé sur les fleurs, au soleil.

5   L'ombre éteignit mes yeux, un cri vint à ma bouche,
Et mon vieux coeur est mort dans un frisson farouche.

Alors le chevalier Malheur s'est rapproché,
Il a mis pied à terre et sa main m'a touché,

Son doigt ganté de fer entra dans ma blessure
10 Tandis qu'il attestait sa loi d'une voix dure.

Et voici qu'au contact glacé du doigt de fer
Un coeur me renaissait, tout un coeur pur et fier.

Et voici que, fervent d'une candeur divine
Tout un coeur jeune et bon battit dans ma poitrine.

15 Or, je restais tremblant, ivre, incrédule un peu,
Comme un homme qui voit des visions de Dieu.

Mais le bon chevalier, remonté sur sa bête,
En s'éloignant, me fit un signe de la tête

---

[20] George Steiner, introducing *The Penguin Book of Modern Verse Translation*, Harmondsworth 1966, p. 28.

[21] Hartwig Schulz, *Vom Rhythmus der modernen Lyrik*, Munich 1970.

Et me cria (j'entends *encore* cette voix):
20 'Au moins, prudence! Car c'est bon pour une fois.'[22]

Vermummter guter reiter auf dem stillen rosse —
Das unglück traf mein altes herz mit dem geschosse.

Mein altes herzensblut in einem strahl entfuhr
Um zu verflüchten in dem lichte auf der flur.

5 Mein aug erlosch·ein schrei entfuhr aus meinem munde·
In wildem zucken ging mein altes herz zugrunde.

Der ritter unglück hat indessen beigelenkt·
Ist abgestiegen·hat die hand auf mich gesenkt.

Sein finger erzumkleidet trat in meine wunde —
10 Er gab mit rauhem wort von seinem willen kunde.

Und sieh! kaum drang sein kalter eisenfinger ein
Ward mir ein neues herz — ein herz so stolz und rein.

Und sieh! erleuchtet wie von einem himmelsdochte
Ein herz so jung und gut in meinem busen pochte.

15 Noch blieb ich zitternd und zum zweifel noch geneigt
Wie einer dem der Herr im Schlaf Gesichte zeigt.

Er aber sass von neuem auf· der gute reiter.
Er nickte mit dem kopf herab und sprengte weiter.

Er schrie: — und seine stimme gellt mir noch im ohr —
20 Nun aber vorsicht! solches kommt nur einmal vor.

---

[22] A good knight, masked, who rides along in silence, / Malfortune has pierced my old heart with his lance.
My old heart's blood gushed out in one vermilion jet, / then steamed away on the flowers, in the sunshine.
Shade extinguished my eyes, a cry rose to my mouth, / And my old heart died with a wild shudder.
Then Sir Malfortune approached, / Set foot on the ground and touched me with his hand,
His iron-gloved finger entered my wound / While he proclaimed his sway with a harsh voice.
And behold — at the icy touch of that iron finger / A heart, pure and proud, was born to me again.
Behold — glowing with divine candour / A heart all young and good beat in my breast.
I stayed trembling then, reeling, a little incredulous / Like a man who sees divine visions.
But the good knight, remounted on his steed, / Nodded to me as he rode away
And cried out to me (in a voice I can still hear): / 'But now — take care! For this can happen only once.'

Verlaine's poem describes a divine warning that induces its recipient to change his life. In a preface to the volume which contains the *Sagesse* cycle Verlaine has himself suggested a parallel between the situation of his 'lyric I' and his own life:

The author of this book has not always thought as he does to-day. He has long wandered in the corruption of our time, and shared in its trespasses and ignorance. Since then he has been warned by well-deserved sorrows, and God has granted him the grace to understand that warning.

The pain of the wound inflicted by Sir Malfortune awakes the central protagonist of the poem to new life; a new heart begins to beat in his breast, 'glowing with divine candour'. He who inflicted the wound and let in this new life calls out a solemn warning as he rides on: there will be no second such miracle — so make the most of this one!

Schulz analyses in great detail the metrical pattern of this poem: the shifting caesuras, the rhythms changing subtly in every line in consonance with story, feeling and mood; and the use of rhythmic *leitmotifs*, notably that associated with the masked knight at the very opening of the poem: x́ xxx́ xx́ (underlined, at its first occurrence, by the internal rhyme '*chevalier-masqué*', and repeated on three further occasions in the poem). Such *leitmotifs* are shown to have their particular tonality and association, and to bind the poem together — some suggesting the marked rider's uncanny, disorientating appearance, others his harshness. . . . Verlaine's lines are *vers libérés*, whose full effect can only be realized by readers who can discern within and behind them other, stricter Alexandrines.

George's translation follows faithfully, line by line, the original's unfolding pattern of story, image and mood; though the necessity of also reproducing the over-all formal and stanzaic pattern inevitably wrings some concessions from him: *lance* becomes the vaguer, more general *geschoss, loi* becomes *wille*. The number of syllables is the same in both versions, so is the rhyme-scheme (down, even, to the sequence of strong and weak endings) — yet the overall rhythmic effect is entirely different. The very opening line suggests the changes to come: Verlaine's relative clause is replaced by a prepositional adjectival phrase, the verb disappears, the nominal construction impedes the rhythmic flow, a static phrase ('auf dem hohen rosse') replaces a dynamic clause ('qui chevauche en silence'); instead of Verlaine's supple changing rhythm we have a strictly controlled iambic one. The forward thrust of the iambs is curbed by the counter-pointing of the 'rising' metre with words that have a 'falling' rhythm, words that end with a weak syllable.

With particular emphasis and effect Schulz juxtaposes the fifteenth line of the two versions:

Or, je restais tremblant, ivre, incrédule un peu . . .

Noch blieb ich zitternd und zum zweifel noch geneigt . . .

Verlaine's line is made up of two occurrences of the rhythmic *leitmotif* already noticed (x́ xxx́ xx́ / x́ xxx́ xx́), which brings an element of restless movement into the line. The words seem to 'swim', as it were — they are only loosely connected syntactically, with many pauses and hesitations; and the sound-colour of the line changes gradually. George tightens up Verlaine's deliberately loose organization in every way possible: through a strict participial construction that does away with the need for hesitating pauses; through more rigidly alternating rhythm; and through a replacement of Verlaine's shifting sound-colouration by a tight network of correspondences. Identical or very similar vowel-sounds and consonants bind contiguous word-groups together (bl*i*eb *i*ch z*i*tternd; *u*nd z*u*m; *z*um *Z*weifel; *n*och ge*n*eigt); these groups, in their turn, are linked with each other through assonances and alliterations, while the two halves into which the line falls are bound together by repetition of the word *noch*. This tight organization is typical of the whole poem in George's version; it renders Verlaine's rhythmic *leitmotif*-technique unnecessary, and George makes, accordingly, no attempt to reproduce it. He will have nothing to do with Verlaine's deliberate 'softening' and 'loosening' of rhythmic and syntactic structure within the syllable-counting tradition of the French Alexandrine — his way is to tighten everything up while playing speech-rhythm against a firmly alternating rhythmic pulse, in the manner of the German verse-tradition (though much more rigidly than anything one could find in Hofmansthal, for instance, or in Rilke).

A comparative analysis such as that attempted by Hartwig Schulz shows clearly the individuality of two very different poets, and also, at the same time, their relation to two very different traditions of composing in verse. The case is the more piquant because George's transformation of what was dynamic and flowing in Verlaine into something more static relates dialectically to the observation made by Albert Malblanc (see above, p. 2) that *German* idiom tends more to the dynamic, and French more to the static.

Closely related to translation studies is the study of adaptations and counter-poems. Yeats's variation on Ronsard's sonnet 'Quand vous serez bien vieille, au soir, à la chandelle' — a poem first published in 1893 which begins with the line 'When you are old and grey and full of sleep' — constitutes a celebrated example of such adaptation, and has been given a model *explication comparative* in Simon Jeune's book *Littérature générale et littérature comparée*.[23] The case of Brecht's dealing with Shelley is equally instructive.

In his search for 'ancestors', for poets who combined sensitivity to language and rhythm with intelligence, social concern and 'progressive' thought, Brecht came across the work of Shelley; and his attention was attracted particularly by *The Masque of Anarchy*, written in 1819, when Shelley had just received news of the killing and wounding, by British soldiers, of a number of workmen who had assembled on St. Peter's Field near Manchester to hear an address on their grievances. The form in which Shelley chose to embody his reaction to the news of 'Peterloo' was a traditional one: a pageant, a triumphal procession like the *Trionfi* of Petrarch, in which the central figure would be, ironically, that very Anarchy which the authorities had sought to vanquish by their show of strength on St. Peter's field. More important, however, than the Petrarchan framework of the poem were Biblical allusions that ran through the whole poem, allusions

[23] Simon Jeune, *Littérature générale et littérature comparée*, Paris 1968, pp. 110-18.

particularly to the Horsemen of the Apocalypse.

Shelley begins his poem on a personal, autobiographical note, referring specifically to his sojourn in Italy where the news of Peterloo reached him. Then follows his vision of the Four Horsemen in modern times: one of them is Anarchy, the others are Murder, Fraud and Hypocrisy. The three last-named appear, in Shelley's poem, in the guise of contemporary statesmen: Murder in the likeness of Castlereagh, then Foreign Secretary, who is attended by the hounds of the Holy Alliance; Fraud in that of Lord Eldon, the Lord Chancellor who had deprived Shelley of the custody of his children; Hypocrisy in that of Lord Sydmouth, the Home Secretary whose responsibility for Peterloo must have seemed particularly grave. This procession is followed by an allegorical presentation of the despair felt by working people whose claims were trampled under foot; Hope herself has become a 'maniac maid' who 'looked more like despair', until in the middle of the poem, through a sudden reversal, Hope arises triumphant, a 'maiden most serene', while Anarchy lies dead. The murdering accomplices of Anarchy are then seen fleeing in terror before the voice of England herself, who affirms her sons' inalienable rights — and Shelley proclaims his panacea, which turns out to be 'non-violent resistance'. Let there be another Peterloo — call another assembly and let the murderers trample you underfoot — and you will see the spirit of England rise up against your oppressors:

And that slaughter to the Nation
Shall steam up like inspiration,
Eloquent, oracular;
A volcano heard afar.

And these words shall then become
Like oppression's thundered doom
Ringing through each heart and brain,
Heard again — again — again —

Rise like lions after slumber
In unvanquishable number —
Shake your chains to earth like dew
Which in sleep had fallen on you —
Ye are many — they are few.

In an essay entitled *The Range and Multiplicity of the Realist Mode of Writing*,[24] Brecht had taken Shelley as his prime example of a writer who expressed himself through symbols and flights of fantasy and yet remained 'concrete' (truth, Brecht had learnt from Hegel, 'is concrete'); whose visionary poems enabled their readers to recognize conflicts in the real world more clearly than they could in the turmoil of living; concerned with formal problems and yet still a 'friend of the people'. In illustration of his thesis, Brecht quoted twenty stanzas of *The Masque of Anarchy* in English and in German translation. Brecht's essay was written in 1938; and nine years later its author felt moved, by what he saw of post-war Germany, to attempt an adaptation of Shelley's poem to modern conditions. The result was *The Anachronistic Procession, or, Freedom and Democracy*. In the original title, it should be noted, the final word is left, ironically, in English: *Der anachronistische Zug oder Freiheit und Democracy*.

Brecht eliminates Shelley's personal introduction: the lyric I, introduced by Shelley in the very opening line, plays no overt part in Brecht's poem at all. Conversely, however, Brecht's opening lines have a more lyrical, singing quality than Shelley's deliberately low-keyed, almost doggerel beginning:

As I lay asleep in Italy,
I heard a voice from over the Sea
And with great power it forth led me . . .

Frühling wurd's in deutschem Land.
Über Asch und Trümmerwand
Flog ein erstes Birkengrün . . .[25]

Unlike Shelley, Brecht refuses to give personal names to present-day embodiments of Murder, Fraud and Anarchy. For Castlereagh, Eldon and Sydmouth he substitutes interest-groups: the Church, industrialists, venal intellectuals, ex-Nazis, cliques of fellow-travellers . . .; and these are joined, when they reach Munich, by six overtly allegorical figures

[24] 'Weite und Vielfalt der realistischen Schreibweise', *Schriften zur Literatur und Kunst* II, *Gesammelte Werke* XIX, Frankfurt 1967, pp. 340-9.

[25] Spring came to the German lands. Over ashes and ruined walls the birches waved their first green . . .

(Oppression, Plague, Fraud, Stupidity, Murder and Robbery) that loudly demand 'Freiheit und Democracy'. There is no peripateia, no 'voice of the country' to speak encouragement — only a hungry and disoriented crowd, watching the procession from the curb-side. In his bitter poem Brecht has in fact *inverted* the structure of Shelley's *Masque*: he begins with hope (a less emphatic hope than that rousingly proclaimed at the end of Shelley's poem; a hope embodied in a landscape picture, the birch-trees putting forth their first new leaves in the German spring-time) and ends with a huge cortège bearing an unknown race to its doom while a chorus of rats creep out of Germany's ruined houses. These rats join the procession and conclude the poem with a piping hurrah for 'Freiheit und Democracy'. Here are the final stanzas of Brecht's poem, to hold against the final stanzas of Shelley's, quoted above; to show how Brecht refuses to amplify the last stanza, to add the extra line and extra rhyme with which Shelley gave such weight, such ringing sonority, to his call for action — a ringing sonority the more striking because of its contrast with the doggerel, broadside-like beginning; to show the drier, less rhetorical, more disillusioned tone of the later poet, and the black humour not found in his model:

Holpernd hinter den sechs Plagen
Fährt ein Riesentotenwagen
Drinnen liegt, man sieht's nicht recht:
's ist ein unbekannt Geschlecht.

Und ein Wind aus den Ruinen
Singt die Totenmesse ihnen
Die dereinst gesessen hatten
Hier in Häusern. Grosse Ratten

Schlüpfen aus gestürzten Gassen
Folgend diesem Zug in Massen.
Hoch die Freiheit, piepsen sie
Freiheit und Democracy![26]

---

[26] Rumbling behind the six plagues / Comes a gigantic hearse. / In it — one can't quite make it out —/ lies an unknown race.
And a wind blowing from the ruins / Sings a requiem mass for those / Who had once sat / In houses here. Large rats
Slither from collapsed streets / Following this procession in droves. / 'Up with Freedom!', they pipe, / 'Freedom and Democracy!'

All Brecht's changes are, of course, deliberate and well considered. They suggest that modern oppressors are 'faceless men', too insignificant in themselves to be named, though strong in association; they appeal to a modern audience, tired of rhetoric and grand gestures, through a bitterly satiric presentation of its own passivity as well as the impudence of those whom Brecht regards as its oppressors; they demonstrate how much, in modern conditions, works against the hope that is nonetheless there, a hope which Brecht here symbolises, as so often, through the image of trees tentatively, delicately and yet boldly putting forth their leaves. Brecht's individuality and the social and political conditions he sought at once to mirror and to change stand out the more clearly by contrast with his acknowledged model: *Der anachronistische Zug* is at once an adaptation of *The Masque of Anarchy* and a counter-poem to it. Since there is no indication, however, that Shelley's style or way of thinking are to be ridiculed, Brecht's poem is in no sense a parody of *The Masque of Anarchy* or a persiflage of its author.

Studies of translation, it need hardly be said, cannot be divorced from study of the theory of translation; a field of which George Watson, in *The Study of Literature*, offers a useful conspectus in briefest compass:

In the first place there are those who have believed, like Horace, Pope and Johnson, that poetry is essentially imitable or translatable in other languages [. . .] In opposition, there are those who consider that it is part of the essential property of poetry to resist translation. Dante, in his *Convivio*, speaks as if this view were widely accepted in his time [. . .] Dryden, in his preface to Juvenal (1693), talks as if looseness were a desperate and yet imperative duty upon the translator, and fidelity to the original a plain impossibility [. . .] Voltaire, in the twenty-first of his *Lettres philosophiques*, speaks of his own 'free translations of the English poets', which he justifies by an appeal to the differing qualities of the two languages [. . .] The great age of the doctrine of poetry as essentially untranslatable is of course the late nineteenth century, and in this age, especially among the French *symbolistes*, language-consciousness achieves its most extreme expression [. . .] In extreme versions of this doctrine, as in the poetry and criticism of Wallace Stevens, language may even be granted the status of a mystical religion in which reality is mediated through the imagination of a poet.[27]

And always, beyond questions of theory as well as of practice, there looms the important question of function. What was it that needed to be translated? What could, what did, translations give to the cultures within which they were produced and assimilated? Graham Hough, in the course of an essay on Rossetti as a translator of Italian poetry, looks back on the earlier history of translation in England:

It is not very important to do in English as a literary exercise what has already been done in English as the expression of first-hand experience. But to reproduce a poetic experience that belongs to another language and that English has never known may be extremely important. From Tudor times to half-way through the eighteenth century this was generally acknowledged. North's *Plutarch* and Pope's *Homer* were among the most influential books of their own periods. From the emergence of the vernaculars to the break-up of European civilisations in our own day translation was one of the most important means of maintaining a common culture. To no country has this been more important than to England, always liable to long spells of insular solitude. Alfred brought to England a selection of Latin Christian literature; Chaucer brought French romance; the Tudor translators a vast collection of classical and Renaissance texts; the Augustans yet more classics, treated with more understanding of their formal qualities; and each of these in their turn fertilised native production.[28]

Here, as elsewhere in comparative literary studies, practical criticism, the study of theory and that of history go hand in hand.

How closely the history of translation and adaptation is in fact linked to that of comparative criticism may be seen from Dryden's Preface to his *Fables*.[29] Dryden had just finished his translation of Ovid's *Metamorphoses*:

Having done with Ovid for this time, it came into my mind, that our old English poet, Chaucer, in many things resembled him, and that with

---

[27] op. cit., London 1969, p. 111. The 'extreme . . . doctrine' of which Watson speaks here was, of course, propounded long before the French Symbolists, and long before Wallace Stevens, by the first German Romantics at the end of the eighteenth and the beginning of the nineteenth century.

[28] Graham Hough, *The Last Romantics*, London 1961, p. 71.

[29] *Fables Ancient and Modern; Translated into Verse from Homer, Ovid, Boccace & Chaucer: with Original Poems*, London 1700.

no disadvantage on the side of the modern author, as I shall endeavour
to prove when I compare them; and as I am, and always have been,
studious to promote the honour of my native country, so I soon
resolved to put their merits to the trial, by turning some of the
Canterbury Tales into our language, as it is now refined; for by this
means, both the poets being set in the same light and dressed in the
same English habit, story to be compared with story, a certain
judgement may be made between them by the reader, without
obtruding my opinion on him.

Chaucer leads Dryden to Boccaccio, and here he does not
hesitate to 'obtrude' his opinion; the Preface to the *Fables*
considers what similarities may be found between the English
and the Italian writer, and speculates on the place they
occupy in literary and linguistic history.

. . . so from Chaucer I was led to think of Boccace, who was not only
his contemporary, but also pursued the same studies; wrote novels in
prose, and many works in verse; particularly is said to have invented the
octave rhyme, or stanza of eight lines, which ever since has been
maintained by the practice of all Italian writers who are, or at least
assume the title of, heroic poets. He and Chaucer, among other things,
had this in common, that they refined their mother-tongues; but with
this difference, that Dante had begun to file their language, at least in
verse, before the time of Boccace, who likewise received no little help
from his master Petrarch; but the reformation of their prose was wholly
owing to Boccace himself, who is yet the standard of purity in the
Italian tongue, though many of his phrases are become obsolete, as in
process of time it must needs happen. Chaucer [. . .] first adorned and
amplified our barren tongue from the Provençal, which was then the
most polished of all the modern languages [. . .] For these reasons of
time, and resemblance of genius, in Chaucer and Boccace, I resolved to
join them in the present work [. . .]

The activities of the translator and adaptor, as Dryden's
preface shows, lead naturally to those of the comparatist
critic and historian of literature.

6.
Themes and Prefigurations

Comparing Brecht's version of a theme and form he found in Shelley (who had himself adapted themes and forms from Petrarch and the Bible) brought us into a domain in which comparatists have always felt very much at home, despite repeated efforts to drive them out of it: that of 'thematics', 'thematology' or *Stoffgeschichte*. Here it will be useful to distinguish five different subjects of investigation, though these will usually combine and overlap, and to give some examples.

(*a*) The literary representation, in different languages and at different times of *natural phenomena* and man's reaction to them: mountains, the ocean, the forest; or of *eternal facts of human existence*: dreams, or death; or of *perennial human problems and patterns of behaviour*: conflict between illusion and reality (from *Don Quixote* to *Madame Bovary*), the power of destiny (from Oedipus at one end to the Sleeping Beauty at the other), the crossing of true love (Hero and Leander, Tristram and Iseult, Romeo and Juliet), libertinage (Don Juan, Casanova).

(*b*) Recurring *motifs* in literature and folklore: the three wishes or three tasks; the Waste Land; the *asiles* of *La nouvelle Héloïse* and *Werther*. Motifs and situations characteristic of folklore and folktale have, in fact, been most thoroughly investigated and classified – notably in Stith Thompson's *Motif-Index of Folk-Literature*.[1]

(*c*) Recurrent *situations* and their treatment by different writers: the eternal triangle, the son resentful of his father, a

---

[1] Stith Thompson, *Motif-Index of Folk-Literature*, 6 vols., 2nd ed. Copenhagen 1955-8.

David confronting a Goliath, two lovers parting at dawn, a
seemingly impossible prophecy fulfilled. The last-quoted
example demonstrates how such 'situations' pass over into
actions. Here one might also add different literary reflections
of the same *historical event*: Byron, Stendhal and Thackeray
evoking the battle of Waterloo, Dickens and Anatole France
the French Revolution, Voltaire and Goethe the Lisbon
earthquake.

(*d*) The literary representation of *types* — professional
groupings, social classes, races, figures incarnating specific
attitudes to life or society: the knight, the commercial
traveller, the urban or agricultural worker, Jewish figures, the
rebel, the criminal, the conformist, the unheroic soldier, the
'superfluous man'.

(*e*) The literary representation of *named personages* from
mythology, legend, earlier literature or history: Prometheus,
say, or Siegfried, or Hamlet, or Napoleon — the names are
legion, and so are the comparative studies — one thinks of
Strich, Walzel, Trousson, E.M. Butler, L. Weinstein, Käte
Hamburger.

Raymond Trousson, who knows the field as thoroughly as
anyone, has argued, persuasively, that the most fruitful
subjects for comparative literary studies will, in fact, be
found under (*e*).[2] It would not be hard, however, to find
interesting and important subjects under (*d*) — the depiction
of criminals and social outcasts in Balzac and Dickens, for
instance,[3] or the image of the social conformist in twentieth-
century English, American and German literature; while a
book like Kurt Wais's *Das Vater-Sohn-Motiv in der Dichtung*
(a discussion and illustration, in two volumes published in
1931, of the way a number of authors writing at various
times had treated the relationship of fathers and sons)
demonstrates that the study of situation and motif can also
yield instructive results to patient and imaginative investiga-

---

[2] See Trousson's 'Playdoyer pour la *Stoffgeschichte*' in *Revue de littérature
comparée* 38 (1964) and his *Un Problème de littérature comparée: les études de
thèmes*, Paris 1965.

[3] '... the devil, the villain, and the criminal — three different sorts of figures,
belonging, respectively, to mythology, melodrama and realism — converge to form
the figure of Fagin (as they did, in different proportions, to form Vautrin) ...'
(Donald Fanger, *Dostoevsky and Romantic Realism*, ed. cit., p. 69).

tors. Here we must, however, take issue once again with a great comparatist who constituted himself the scourge of other comparatists. Benedetto Croce denied uncompromisingly that there is any significant connection between figures with common names, and fables with common outlines, to be found in the work of different writers. If Trissino, Corneille, Voltaire and Alfieri compose plays which all centre on the figure of Sophonisba, then — Croce maintains — the true protagonist is not the daughter of Hasdrubal who lends her name, and the outline of her fate, to all the plays alike; the true protagonist is rather the creative personality of each separate poet who has given to the old figure and fable its new shape and content. Yet it is precisely Croce's argument, it seems to me, which justifies a comparative study of the four Sophonisba-plays: a sensitive and perceptive analysis of four works that have at least an outline in common will throw into stronger relief the creative personality of each writer and his cultural ambience. K.A.J. Batterby has found himself able to throw light on the different personalities of Gide and Rilke, for instance, by examining the way each of them used the parable of the Prodigal Son. Gide, he tells us,

like Rilke, was a great traveller and hungry for experience; each could find in the story of the Prodigal Son something which matched a part of himself. But Gide's Prodigal Son returned — and was glad to return — because his 'aspirations were thwarted and finally tamed by dangers and hardships' [E.M. Butler], because his courage and endurance were not sufficient to sustain him. Of Rilke's, on the other hand, we read: 'Wir wissen nicht, ob er blieb; wir wissen nur, dass er wiederkam'[4] — the inference, based on Rilke's conception of the parable, surely being that there could be no permanent return. The implication in the closing lines of *Malte* is unmistakably that the resumption of normal family life was impossible. This leads us to the essential contrast between Rilke and Gide. The latter, for all his journeying and adventure, was firmly rooted in his own soil and home. He belonged inseparably to the environment and conditions from which he originated; there was no intention or desire to sever those ties. His travels were merely an interlude, and he returned from them exhausted and satisfied, ready to resume his normal existence where it had been interrupted. For Rilke is was not even a question of travelling; it was one of *exile*, of complete severance, a social and domestic withdrawal

---

[4] 'We do not know whether he stayed; all we know is that he came back.'

which was absolute. For him the problem was altogether deeper, bound up indissolubly with his whole approach to life and with his dedication to his calling: his Prodigal Son is the symbol of his belief that his art was paramount and that there was no room for two loyalties. Where, for Gide, absence from country and home was no more than a temporary fructifying experience, for Rilke it was an article of faith, allowing no compromise or retracing of steps.[5]

Such studies of theme and motif may be seen as the literary equivalent of what art-historians know as iconography; and its interest seems to me assured by at least three considerations.

First: the comparative study of themes and motifs enables us to see what type of writer chooses what type of material, and how the material is dealt with at various times. Elisabeth Frenzel, whose comparative dictionary of themes and personages[6] is an indispensable tool for such studies, has demonstrated how some writers (Hans Sachs, for instance) will find any theme grist to a somewhat coarsely grinding mill; how others (Rotrou, for example, or Herder) ferret out interesting themes but leave it to others to make the most of them; how others again (Shakespeare is the most notable though not the only instance) have a genius for combining themes and motifs from the most varied sources and integrating them into unified works of art; how yet others (Racine, for example, or Hofmannsthal) weigh and filter and distil their themes. Nor is it idle to ask what writers as different from each other as Dante, Machiavelli and Shakespeare saw in the figure of Brutus; how their conceptions of Brutus relate to those of Robespierre, Saint-Just and Heine. Such questions should interest students of literature no less than students of society and political ideas.

'Thematic' studies enable us, in fact, to examine and contrast the spirit of different societies and epochs as well as those of individual talents. It is fascinating to see how the problems facing groups, classes and societies become embodied in literary figures with a life and an individuality of

---

[5] K.A.J. Batterby, *Rilke and France: A Study in Poetic Development*, Oxford 1966, p. 135.

[6] *Stoffe der Weltliteratur: Ein Lexikon dichtungsgeschichtlicher Längsschnitte*, 3rd (revised) edition, Stuttgart 1970.

their own and, at the same time, a representative quality that wins recognition throughout Europe and beyond: Werther, Raskolnikov, the 'superfluous man', the Outsider. . . . It is fascinating, also, to see stories going back to classical Greek and Roman times assimilated in varying ways to the chivalrous ideal of the Middle Ages or the humanist ideal of the eighteenth century; to see them recreated by nineteenth-century historicism or reinterpreted by twentieth-century psychologising. Nor is it an unimportant or time-wasting exercise to examine the popularity of different themes at different times and speculate on the social, political and cultural reasons for their ups and downs. When and why, Harry Levin has forcibly asked,[7] did the story of Troilus and Cressida have a special vogue? Why was Hebbel, why was Wagner, attracted to the Nibelungen theme — and what attracted their audiences to attend performances of the resulting works? This kind of study can make an important contribution to the history of ideas; a history which is indissolubly connected with that of literature.

Lastly: thematic studies must not be divorced from study of literary style. Different motifs — Dámaso Alonso had to remind E.R. Curtius — may have different stylistic casts. Nor must it be abstracted from the study of literary genre — as Ulrich Weisstein has well said, we have only to look at the selection the tragic poets of classical Greece made from the corpus of legends that deals with the Trojan wars to see how aware *they* must have been of the suitability of given themes for given genres. A useful investigation along these lines has recently been attempted by Volker Klotz in a book on the novel and the big city.[8] Klotz there examines the way in which the 'city' theme has attracted novelists in many European countries from Lesage to Döblin; he tries to demonstrate, with some success, that there is an affinity between the form of the novel and the theme of the multi-stranded, confusing, many-voiced city of modern times.

---

[7] Harry Levin's rehabilitation of *Stoffgeschichte* appeared, appropriately, in a *Festschrift* for René Wellek: *The Disciplines of Criticism*, ed. Demetz, Greene and Nelson, New Haven 1968. Levin's essay is entitled 'Thematics and Criticism'.

[8] Volker Klotz, *Die erzählte Stadt*, Munich 1969.

Our own century has been especially fertile in attempts to pour old wines into new bottles — particularly in its re-interpretation of classical myths and more modern legends embodied in literary works of the past. The most eloquent call to examine this phenomenon has come from Raymond Trousson, who has pronounced such studies 'a difficult exercise, as far removed from dusty erudition as from the scope of beginners in criticism, a task often demanding and arduous, sometimes ungrateful, but ever invigorating and new, revealing something of the secret, strong life of the great figures we have made, century after century, our own glorious doubles'.[9] According to Trousson, the study of recurrent figures and figurations aims at 'finding, across many reincarnations of a single hero, some constants, some fundamental problems, in a word: something essential to human nature, something ceaselessly modified yet always preserved and transmitted beneath this mythic guise'.[10] There have been several valuable comparative studies of this kind. These include Trousson's own book on the Prometheus theme in European literature[11] and Käte Hamburger's study of the fortunes of Greek heroes in plays from Sophocles to Sartre.[12]   Käte Hamburger concentrates on the meta-morphoses of literary figures without taking account of the different structures of the plays in which they occur; her book is therefore more lopsided than John White's *Mythology in the Modern Novel*, which also discusses the differing structural functions of the myths and techniques discussed. White distinguishes subtly and usefully between works that re-narrate a classical myth; works that juxtapose sections narrating a myth with others that concern themselves with the modern world; works which, while being set in the modern world, have a pattern of mythological references running through them; and works containing a mythological

---

[9] Raymond Trousson, *Un Problème de littérature comparée: les études de thèmes*, Paris 1965.

[10] 'Playdoyer pour la *Stoffgeschichte'*, *Revue de littérature comparée* 38 (1963).

[11] Trousson, *Le Thème de Prométhée dans la littérature européenne*, Geneva 1964.

[12] *Von Sophokles zu Sartre: Griechische Dramenfiguren antik und modern*, Stuttgart 1962.

motif that prefigures part of the narrative, but does not run consistently through it. This classification is supported by many comparisons of novels in different languages which (refreshingly) do not shrink from aesthetic judgments:

A mythological novel is largely successful when it manages to present the reader with an important literary theme and at the same time makes him feel the chosen analogy has enriched his understanding of the primary material. When the reader feels the contemporary subject and the mythological motif are ill matched, when the prefiguration either appears to be gratuitously pretentious or unnecessarily obscure, the mythology is clearly not serving any aesthetically useful purpose. Viewed in these terms, Joyce's *Ulysses* and Michael Butor's *L'Emploi du temps* are novels that make extensive and effective use of their mythological analogies; Anthony Burgess's *A Vision of Battlements* and Geno Hartlaub's *Nicht jeder ist Odysseus* involve a less happy handling of the same device — largely because one does not feel that the prefiguration has added much to the novel. Elizabeth Langgässer's *Märkische Argonautenfahrt* conveys a rather banal mythological scheme; yet in Macdonald Harris's *Trepleff* what might have been an equally facile system of analogies is exploited to some comic effect. In fact, the mood in which correspondences are presented in almost as important as their ramifications.[13]

What appears here as apodictic judgment is backed up in every instance by reasoned analysis and comparison elsewhere in the book.

By using mythological plots and prefigurative techniques (and by introducing quotations and allusions), writers invite their readers to make comparisons, to become comparatists. One cannot fully appreciate Goethe's *Iphigenie auf Tauris* without testing, for oneself, how it differs from Euripides' play on the same theme, or Anouilh's *Antigone* without mental reference to Sophocles. Without our recollection of the old story and the old play Anouilh could not achieve the Pirandellian effect he aims at by making his Antigone and his Creon aware that they are performing preordained parts. The ambiguous way in which he distributes his sympathies have led some to see his play as an apology for fascism, others as an expressive of the spirit of the Resistance;[14] and Käte

---

[13] John White, *Mythology in the Modern Novel: A Study of Prefigurative Techniques*, pp. 90-1.

[14] The different interpretations are well summarised and documented in W.M. Landers' edition of Anouilh's *Antigone*, London 1954, pp. 15-29.

Hamburger has argued, with some justice, that Anouilh's play may make us take a fresh look at that of Sophocles and discover in the old Antigone the seeds of a death-wish more strongly expressed by the new.[15] The speeches of Anouilh's heroine of 1944 make an interesting contrast, too, with the monologue put into Antigone's mouth by a Polish poet writing in 1949 — a monologue that restores the rebellious, anti-tyrannical implications of the old story which no amount of Hegelian exegesis, or of Anouilhan ambiguity, has ever been able to annul:

> These are not only words, Ismene, not only.
> Kreon cannot build his empire
> Upon our graves. He will not be able
> To establish here his order with the naked sword.
> The might of the dead is great. Nobody
> Is ever protected from them. Let him
> Surround himself with a crowd of spies
> And millions of guards, they will find him
> Everywhere. The hours are waiting,
> They tread ironically around the madman
> Who does not believe in them.[16]

Such implicit or explicit comparisons can sometimes help us arrive at aesthetic judgments: remembrances of Sophocles forced upon us by O'Neill's *Mourning Becomes Electra* reveal all too clearly the dull ordinariness of O'Neill's neurotic characters and the inadequacy of his language to his great theme. They can also help us to appreciate the different possibilities of different modes and conventions at different times: the terrifying description of the Erinyes and their song in Aeschylus's *Eumenides* and Ovid's *Metamorphoses* contrasts with T.S. Eliot's unhappy attempt to introduce similar figures into the modern world of *The Family Reunion*:

They must, in future, be omitted from the cast, and be understood to be visible only to certain of my characters, and not to the audience. We tried every possible manner of presenting them. We put them on the stage and they looked like uninvited guests who had strayed in from a

---

[15] cf. Käte Hamburger, *Von Sophocles zu Sartre*, ed. cit., pp. 192-212.

[16] Czeslaw Milosz, *Kontynenty*, Paris 1958, p. 365. The translation is by George Gömöri and comes from Gömöri's book *Polish and Hungarian Poetry 1945 to 1956*, Oxford 1966, pp. 43-4.

fancy-dress ball. We concealed them behind gauze, and they suggested a still out of a Walt Disney film. We made them dimmer, and they looked like shrubbery just outside the window. I have seen other expedients tried: I have seen them signalling from across the garden, or swarming on the stage like a football team, and they are never right. They never succeed in being either Greek goddesses or modern spooks. But their failure is merely a symptom of the failure to adjust the ancient with the modern.[17]

Despite the failure which Eliot has thus diagnosed in his own play with a characteristic rueful acuteness, one suspects that more could be made of his Eumenides-figures now that so many younger stage-directors have experimented with various forms of stylization and secularized ritual.

The necessity for constant mental comparison between the new work and the old is all the greater, of course, when there is deliberate inversion or parody of one or more previous treatments of a theme. This happens in Max Frisch's play *Don Juan or the Love of Geometry*, which shows its eponymous hero pushed against his will into the role of the great lover, when all he wants is to stay quietly at home and study mathematics; or in Sartre's *The Flies*, where a swarm of flies replaces the Furies, and where Oreste defies Jupiter by taking guilt freely upon himself, knowing that to do so is 'absurd' — Oreste, in fact, demonstrates his 'freedom' by not seeking purification of his guilt; or in Joyce's *Ulysses*, where the Penelope-figure turns out to be *un*faithful. *Ulysses* shows us clearly the two main modes in which older works can be co-present in modern ones: as ironic counterpoint, and as 'prefiguration', a term whose usefulness John J. White has admirably demonstrated.

Although now frequent in literary criticism, the word 'prefiguration' is of religious origin, a translation of the Latin technical term *figura* used to describe the scheme by which 'the persons and events of the Old Testament were prefigurations of the New Testament and its history of Salvation' [Erich Auerbach]. One of the classic examples of prefiguration in this sense is the prophetic relationship between Abraham's preparation to sacrifice his son Isaac and the Crucifixion. In St. Augustine's time, the word *praefiguratio* was used instead of *figura* and since then the term has been secularized and adapted to many other

---

[17] Quoted in George Steiner's *The Death of Tragedy*, London 1961, p. 329.

contexts. Obviously, when used in the secular sense, the idea of prefiguration loses its original prophetic connotation. In the literary context, Homer's *Odyssey* can hardly be interpreted as a joyous or foreboding prophecy that Joyce's *Ulysses* was to come.

One merit of the term 'prefiguration' in its secularized sense is its latitude of meaning. With it, one can enlarge the scope of an investigation of such symbolic correspondences, to avoid certain misconceptions, by treating not only motifs taken from old mythologies, but also those using legends. For example, the legendary motif of Faust and the devil in John Hersey's *Too Far to Walk* is structurally very similar to many mythological motifs. A wider term also makes it possible to compare mythological motifs with literary plot-prefigurations, such as the use of Shakespeare's plays in Aldous Huxley's *Brave New World*. . .[18]

and, one might add, the use of Shakespeare's *Hamlet* in Alfred Döblin's *Hamlet, or, The Long Night comes to an End.* The very names of characters and vessels in *Moby Dick* invite comparisons with the earlier Ishmael, the wanderer and outcast, or with the earlier Ahab, who worshipped Baal and provoked the Lord to anger, or with Rachel weeping for her children.[19] As for the methods of *Ulysses*: T.S. Eliot drew attention to their importance for the whole of modern literature in his review of the book, a review entitled *Ulysses, Order and Myth*:[20]

Mr. Joyce's parallel use of the *Odyssey* [. . .] has the importance of a scientific discovery. No one else has built a novel upon such a foundation before: it has never before been necessary [. . .] Instead of the narrative method we may use the mythical method. It is, I seriously believe, a step toward making the modern world possible for art . . .

and again, in a notorious passage from the same review:

In using the myth, in manipulating a continuous parallel between contemporaneity and antiquity, Mr. Joyce is pursuing a method which others must pursue after him [. . .] It is simply a way of controlling, of ordering, of giving a shape and a significance to the immense panorama of futility and anarchy which is contemporary history.

---

[19] cf. Harry Levin, *The Power of Blackness*, New York 1958, p. 12.

[18] White, op. cit., pp. 12-13.

[20] *The Dial*, November 1923.

No wonder, then, that Eliot's own *Waste Land* is full of prefigurative patterns, and full also of allusions to and snatches from many earlier works of literature. A comparative approach is thus almost inevitable, though we must not make the mistake of supposing that the use of a single snatch from the work of an earlier poet implies a knowledge of the whole output of that poet and the whole tradition in which he stands.[21] Scholars must not, in other words, be tempted to remake poets in their own image. Eliot has himself gently rebuked some of his interpreters for such misunderstanding at the opening of his essay *The Classics and the Man of Letters*:

In my earlier years I obtained, partly by subtlety, partly by effrontery, and partly by accident, a reputation among the credulous for learning and scholarship, of which (having no further use for it) I have since tried to disembarrass myself. Better to confess one's weaknesses, when they are certain to be revealed sooner or later, than to leave them to be exposed to posterity: though it is, as I have discovered, easier in our times to acquire an undeserved reputation for learning than to get rid of it.

Here, as everywhere in literary investigation, the comparatist needs a sense of proportion, and a sense of the difference between the creative processes of an author and the burrowings of the research-worker.

Related to the re-interpretations and inversions of the traits of named characters (Ulysses, Antigone, Don Juan, Faust) is the creation of what one might call *anti-types*. The young woman with whom Goethe's Werther falls in love captured the imagination of a whole generation of readers not least because she was conceived as the direct antithesis of the feminine ideal propagated by Richardson and his successors. Many who admired her did so in reaction against adulation of the type of heroine describe by Ian Watt as 'very inexperienced, and so delicate in physical and mental constitution that she faints at any sexual advance; essentially passive, she is devoid of any feelings towards her admirers

[21] This fallacy is admirably discussed in T.J. Reed's essay 'Thomas Mann and Tradition: Some Clarifications', in *The Discontinuous Tradition: Studies in German Literature in Honour of Ernest Ludwig Stahl*, ed. P.F. Ganz, Oxford 1971.

until the marriage knot is tied'.[22] Lotte's union of robust-
ness, good sense and sensibility, her combination of sexual
attractiveness and motherly efficiency, made a refreshing
change — but it also drew down the ridicule of a later
generation:

> Charlotte, having seen his body
>   Borne before her on a shutter,
> Like a well-conducted person
>   Went on cutting bread and butter.[23]

It is interesting to recall that in his portrait of Amelia in *Vanity
Fair*, the author of these irreverent verses also threw ironic
sidelights on the Richardsonian ideal which had survived into
the nineteenth century.

The study of themes, situations and motifs must, like all
literary study, keep itself aware of individual variations on
the one hand and wider cross-connections on the other.
Werner Vordtriede, in his book on the relation of French
Symbolism to German Romanticism,[24] discusses a whole
constellation of motifs common to the two movements —
motifs which include subterranean realms, artificial gardens
and the creation of artificial men. Each of these, Vordtriede
demonstrates, gains by being seen together with the other
and with their anti-types. Even the mere listing of such
motifs suggests that there are links here between literature
and folk-lore, between highly refined products of nineteenth
century writers and the *Märchen* or *contes de fées* produced in
earlier, less sophisticated societies — tales preserved through
oral tradition and through volumes compiled by collectors and
adapters. Works which investigate these connections and
compare the treatment of given motifs in folk-tales with
treatment of the same motif in more subtly organized and
individualized texts — like Max Lüthi's *Volksliteratur und
Hochliteratur*[25] — can be valuable contributions to
comparative literary studies. Lüthi's detailed examination of

---

[22] Ian Watt, *The Rise of the Novel: Studies in Defoe, Richardson and Fielding*,
Harmondsworth 1963, p. 167.

[23] W.M. Thackeray, *The Sorrows of Werther*.

[24] Werner Vordtriede, *Novalis und die französischen Symbolisten*, Stuttgart 1963.

[25] Max Lüthi, *Volksliteratur und Hochliteratur*, Bern 1970.

the way a simple motif (transporting a large number of sheep one by one across a narrow bridge) is varied in a folk-tale, in one of Mozart's letters (28 February 1778) and in *Don Quixote* (Part 1, chapter 20), demonstrates how fruitful it can be to examine literary works in a context which includes not only folklore, but also such utilitarian forms as a private letter not intended for publication.

Here we have come close, once again, to the realm of myth and archetype which links literature with ritual and dream.

If archetypes are communicable symbols, and there is a centre of archetypes, we should expect to find, at that centre, a group of universal symbols. I do not mean by this phrase that there is any archetypal code book which has been memorized by all known societies without exception. I mean that some symbols are images of things common to all men, and therefore have a communicable power which is potentially unlimited. Such symbols include those of food and drink, of the quest or journey, of light and darkness, and of sexual fulfilment, which would usually take the form of marriage. It is inadvisable to assume that an Adonis or Oedipus myth is universal, or that certain associations, such as the serpent with the phallus, are universal, because when we discover a group of people who know nothing of such matters we must assume that they did know and have forgotten, or do know and won't tell, or are not members of the human race. On the other hand, they may be confidently excluded from the human race if they cannot understand the conception of food, and so any symbolism founded on food is universal in the sense of having an indefinitely extensive scope. That is, there are no limits to its intelligibility.[26]

Comparatists must take account of symbols and symbol-systems of this kind, though this does not commit them to notions of 'inherited racial memories' or to Jungian psychology. What they must never leave in doubt, however, is the centrality of their interest in literature; interest in individual works which show great writers using, varying and combining types, themes, motifs, situations and myths. What counts, in the end, is the specific, the individual note, the special variation, the fresh nuance. Much is gained, Philip Wheelwright has said, if we see the theme of 'Hidden Power' at the heart of both *Measure for Measure* and *The Tempest*:

But what a pallid, thin idea is the conceptual universal, 'hidden power',

---

[26] Northrop Frye, *Anatomy of Criticism: Four Essays*, Princeton 1957, p. 118.

as compared with the richly developed archetype, a part of whose essential meaning involves in the one case the brothels of Vienna, the hypocrisy of proclaimed purity, the comedy-cliché of the bed-trick, and the uneasy justification of 'craft against vice'; in the other case the music that creeps by upon the waters, the ambivalent mystery of sleep and dream, and the three levels (Prospero, Ariel, Ferdinand) of confinement groping for freedom.[27]

If it is wrong to think of authors and their works as so many discrete points in an orderless cultural universe,[28] it is no less wrong to see only what is general and neglect what is individual, to see only systems and constellations and disregard the particularity of its constituents.

It should be recognized, however, that the study of themes and motifs, like so many of the comparatist's most distinctive activities, can become history of ideas without losing its status as *literary* history and criticism. Harald Weinrich's essay on the way various eighteenth-century writers introduced the Lisbon earthquake into their works provides a telling example.[29] Weinrich discusses the roles of Leibniz, Pope, Lessing, Goethe, Voltaire and Rousseau in the great eighteenth-century debate about the place of evil in the world-order; he shows why the motif of the earthquake should have so persistently commended itself to authors concerned to justify the ways of God to man; and he demonstrates how the same motif is introduced, with differing function and emphasis, into other literary versions of the same debate from the Book of Job to Kleist's *Earthquake in Chile* and Brecht's *Five Difficulties in Writing the Truth*. He demonstrates, concretely, how in each case a

---

[27] Philip Wheelwright, *The Burning Fountain: A Study in the Language of Symbolism*, rev. ed., Bloomington 1968, p. 84.

[28] 'The concern of the historian is with the fact that a poem or a novel has belonged to an organized whole considered as a historical occurrence and thus been brought into one of the 'orders' that societies strive to build. Insofar as it did so belong, the individual work of art did not merely become an additional unit in a sum of separate units. It entered a structural whole, a system, among those parts significant and reciprocal relations existed. The inability to perceive these relations is what one might term the 'atomistic fallacy' in literary studies.' Claudio Guillén, *Literature as System*, Princeton 1971, p. 5.

[29] Harald Weinrich, 'Literaturgeschichte eines Weltereignisses: Das Erdbeben von Lissabon', *Literatur für Leser: Essays und Aufsäize zur Literaturwissenschaft*, Stuttgart 1971.

distinctive literary achievement, or an equally distinctive intellectual argument, is fully intelligible only against a historical background which may include such things as a specific earthquake at a specific time, the reception of an English poem and a German philosophic work in France, a competition set by the Prussian Academy of Sciences, and the distinction, recently refined, between natural, moral and metaphysical evil. In the course of this examination Weinrich finds himself compelled to analyse the narrative perspective his authors adopt (how Goethe, for instance, in his auto-biography, merges the perspectives of the 1750s with that of 1811) and also the different ways in which the common 'earthquake' motif is integrated into the structure of a number of literary works. He is therefore justified in claiming, by his very title, that his essay is a contribution to *literary* history as well as to the history of ideas.

7.
Genres, Movements, Periods

Genre studies, it has been said, are of special interest to comparatists because they combine literary history and literary theory in an international context.[1] They may usefully go in two different directions. They may move towards abstraction: towards seeing what it is that unites plays as different as *Oedipus Tyrannos, Phèdre, King Lear, Maria Magdalena* ... sufficiently to allow us to posit an entity called 'tragedy'. An indispensable aid in this process of abstraction will be the notion of 'family resemblances' — we need not look for one property that all the instances have in common, but must try to discover a series of resemblances that unite them all in the way family likenesses bind together a family: 'Some of them have the same nose, others the same eyebrows and others again the same way of walking; and these likenesses overlap.'[2] The other direction such studies may usefully take is towards differentiation; and this can assume many forms. We may examine the history of tragedy in two different countries at the same period, in order to see how the notion changes in both. We may examine the different concepts of a *novella* or *nouvelle* held by eminent

[1] Ulrich Weisstein, *Vergleichende Literaturwissenschaft*, ed. cit., p. 148.

[2] Ludwig Wittgenstein, *The Blue and Brown Books*, Oxford 1964, p. 17. cf. Robert C. Elliot, 'The Definition of Satire', *Yearbook of Comparative and General Literature* XI (1962), p. 23: 'How does one know whether x (which perhaps seems a kind of borderline case) is a satire or not? Following Wittgenstein, one looks at a number of satires about which there is no question — which are all the centre of the concept, so to speak — and then decides whether work x has resemblances enough to the undoubted examples of the type to be included in it. The point is: this is not a *factual* question to be settled by examining the work for the necessary and sufficient properties which would automatically entitle it to the name *satire*; this is a *decision* question: are the resemblances of this work to various kinds of satire sufficient so that we are warranted in including it in the category — or in extending the category to take it in?'

practitioners like Boccaccio, Cervantes and Margaret of Navarre, as well as such historical continuity as may be seen in this sequence of concepts. We may examine the differing relations between theory and practice in a wide context; contrasting, for instance, the position suggested by J. Brandt Corstius:

The idea of genre and the principle of mutual order of the genres ranked high in Western literary criticism between 1500 and 1800: to plan a literary work was to choose one or another genre; to criticize a poem or a piece of prose was to judge it by the well-defined and generally acknowledged criteria of the genre to which the author asserted his work belonged to.[3]

with that suggested by Tzvetan Todorov when describing our own time:

It is doubtful whether contemporary literature is altogether exempt from distinction into genres; but these distinctions no longer correspond to the notions left to us by the literary theory of the past.[4]

Or we may examine the relation of theory and practice in a more limited context, as Walter Pabst does in a useful work on the *novella* in Italy, Spain and France.[5] Pabst chronicles many struggles between theory, tradition, 'rules' and the creative imagination, and examines the work of authors who say 'Yes' to the traditions of their genre and the often prescriptive theories they find; those who say 'No', rebel against them, try to do away with them or modify them substantially; and those who pay lip-service to a theory their work transcends or denies.

In other ways, too, genre-studies operate at differing levels of generalization and abstraction. On the most general level there are books like Emil Staiger's *Basic Concepts in Poetics*[6] in which the adjectives 'lyric', 'epic' and 'dramatic' are said to

[3] J. Brandt Corstius, *Introduction to the Comparative Study of Literature*, New York 1968, p. 82.

[4] Tzvetan Todorov, *Introduction à la littérature fantastique*, Paris 1970, p. 12.

[5] *Novellentheorie und Novellendichtung: Zur Geschichte ihrer Antinomie in den romanischen Literaturen*. 2nd (revised) edition, Heidelberg 1967. This book contains a welcome demonstration of the fluidity of terms like *novella, nouvelle* and *Novelle*, and the danger of hypostatizing the types of story they represent apart from their realization in the work of specific authors.

[6] Emil Staiger, *Grundbegriffe der Poetik*, 3rd ed., Zürich 1956.

imply constant human attitudes to the world and to time. Staiger tries to find 'pure' examples of each (German Romantic lyrics, Homer's epics, Kleist's plays); for the most part, however, he follows the example of Goethe, who saw them as co-present, in different degrees, in one and the same work of art — who saw lyric, epic and dramatic elements in every successful ballad, for instance. This unhistorical approach has not, despite its sanction by Goethe, proved a great deal of use in literary criticism; it enters remarkably little into the patient and sensitive *explications de texte* which are Staiger's greatest contributions to the study of literature.[7]

At a lower level of generalization one finds studies, not of 'lyric', 'epic' and 'dramatic' but of *the* lyric, *the* epic and — increasingly — *the* novel, seen at first as a sub-genre of 'epic' but later as a genre of its own. Further sub-divisions at once suggest themselves. Discussions of the drama divide themselves from the first, from Aristotle onwards, into discussions of 'tragedy' and 'comedy', classified according to the matter as well as the manner of imitation; and within the lyric (which Aristotle did not recognize as a separate genre at all) discussions of the ode, the elegy, the sonnet and so on are legion. Within these again further sub-divisions may be distinguished; for a brief and telling example, we might turn to the case of the pastoral elegy.

The history of the pastoral goes back to Theocritus, a highly cultured poet who stylized, in his poetry, the life of Sicilian goatherds and shepherds. His stylizations appealed to later Roman poets, notably Virgil, who in their turn stylized not so much the lives of Italian shepherds as the creations of Theocritus. Within this pastoral convention another grew up, one which looked for inspiration less to Theocritus than to two poets roughly contemporary with him: Bion, the author of an elegy entitled *Lament for Adonis*, and Moschus, who wrote a *Lament for Bion*. Moschus's poem is particularly interesting — for here we have yet another kind of stylization, transforming a specific poet, Bion, into the kind of shepherd he wrote about. This was the tradition of pastoral elegy

[7] 'Our test of the adequacy of any aesthetic theory is the criteria it offers in the aid of practical criticism of the various arts.' Morris Weitz, *Philosophy on the Arts*, Cambridge, Mass., 1950, p. 34.

which Milton found ready to his purpose when faced with the task of commemorating his friend Edward King, who had been his fellow-student at Cambridge and who had died at sea. It was this tradition too, enriched by Milton's *Lycidas* and Shelley's *Adonais*, which Matthew Arnold found appropriate when he tried to commemorate his poet-friend Arthur Hugh Clough. The pleasure to be derived from *Lycidas*, and from Arnold's *Thyrsis*, is one of seeing grief, recollected happiness and concern about contemporary events at once expressed and distanced; of seeing a strongly marked personality like Milton's adapt itself to a tradition and at the same time bend tradition to its purposes; of finding the conventions of Greek and Latin poetry, which Milton, Arnold and many of their readers knew intimately, merging with native English traditions without incongruity.

This view — that there is no incongruity in Milton's marriage of classical conventions and English modes of feeling — has been vigorously challenged, of course, by Dr Johnson, whose attack on *Lycidas*, in his *Life of Milton*, amounts to a condemnation of the pastoral tradition in English poetry. Johnson's views are discussed and gently refuted by Lionel Elvin, who has nevertheless seen the justice and relevance of the questions Johnson has raised:

The question we have to answer is whether, in a given case, there is congruity enough between the artifice imposed by the tradition and the actual experience of the poet. The congruity needs to be between fiction and fact in both the personal relationship and the setting. For instance, if a business-man in Chicago with a turn for traditional verse (there may conceivably be such) were to write a pastoral elegy to commemorate one of his business partners we should all be a little unconvinced. Chicago, 'hog-butcher to the world', may be an exciting city, and its exponents of the virtue of 'private enterprise' may have great vigour, but to ask the reader to accept it as the setting for an elegy in the tradition of the Greek Sicilian poets would be too much. A certain degree of adaptation is of course possible. Virgil may have described the countryside of Theocritus, and his peasants, more than those of Tuscany; but no great violence was done. Matthew Arnold in *Thyrsis* may have described the Oxford country, but that was by no means an inadequate alternative. So long as the setting in actuality has reasonable congruity with the shepherd theme then the convention may work perfectly well.[8]

---

[8] Lionel Elvin, *Introduction to the Study of Literature*, London 1949, vol. I, pp. 66-7. The insights afforded by this stimulating book have been used throughout the above discussion of pastoral elegy.

Elvin shows similar 'congruities' between the thoughts and experiences to be conveyed by *Lycidas* and *Thyrsis* and those that animated the poetry of Bion, Moschus and Virgil.

Pastoral elegy, like other genres, has no Platonic idea laid up in heaven. Its study, like all genre-study, must be historical, examining developments and modifications in an international, inter-linguistic context. Each new work at once enriches the tradition and changes it. At the same time, however, genre-study must be theoretical, must examine and define the formal characteristics without which a given work would cease to belong to a specific genre. This point is made with great force by Wellek and Warren, in the excellent chapter they devote to the question of genre in their *Theory of Literature*. 'Formal characteristics' may mean many things:

Genre should be conceived, we think, as a grouping of literary works based, theoretically, upon both outer form (specific metre or structure) and also upon inner form (attitude, tone, purpose — more crudely, subject and audience). The ostensible basis may be one or the other (e.g. 'pastoral' and 'satire' for the inner form; dipodic verse and Pindaric ode for outer); but the critical problem will then be to find the *other* dimension, to complete the diagram.

Sometimes an instructive shift occurs: 'elegy' starts out in English as well as in the archetypal Greek and Roman poetry with the elegiac couplet or distich; yet the ancient elegiac writers did not restrict themselves to lament for the dead, nor did Hammond and Shenstone, Gray's predecessors. But Gray's 'Elegy', written in the heroic quatrain, not in couplets, effectively destroys any continuation in English of elegy as a tender personal poem written in end-stopped couplets.[9]

Wellek and Warren are thus aware of the difficulty of 'completing the diagram', particularly from the eighteenth entury onwards; but their defence of genre-criticism is justified by the work of many modern comparatists, from Carol Madison's *Apollo and the Nine: A History of the Ode*, London 1960, and T.R. Henn's *The Harvest of Tragedy*, London 1966, to Tzvetan Todorov's recent examinations of Boccaccio's *novelle* and the fantastic *contes* of the nineteenth century. There have been valuable studies, too, on an

---

[9] Wellek and Warren, *Theory of Literature*, 3rd ed., Harmondsworth 1963, pp. 232-3.

international basis, of devices peculiar to one genre or another — Wayne Booth's *The Rhetoric of Fiction*,[10] though over-elaborate, makes important distinctions between various narrative techniques and points of view in the European and North American novel. In all these works genre is seen as something Harry Levin has called an 'institution':[11] something that evolves historically, something aspiring writers find ready to hand, something they can work within or try to widen or disrupt or transcend.

Studies of the traditional genres must be supplemented by studies of forms that are not purely literary; forms like the Essay (from Bacon to, say, Hofmannsthal); the diary, from Herder's *Journal* of 1769 to Amiel and thence to Gide, Kafka and Pavese; historiography, biography and autobiography. Roy Pascal's study of the last-named[12] has shown that such non-fictional forms have laws of their own which can be discovered by judicious collocations and comparisons of authors writing in many countries and many languages. How closely utilitarian forms like the private letter are connected with literary forms, fashions and structures has been demonstrated many times: nowhere more forcibly than in Ian Watt's discussion[13] of the eighteenth-century cult of letter-writing, with its roots in economic and social developments and improvements in communications; of the changing style of the letter in the eighteenth century, with its implications of subjective, individualist and private orientations in eighteenth-century life; and of the connection between the private letters of the day with those in the great epistolary novels from Richardson's *Pamela* to Goethe's *Werther*.

For the study of literary movements, and of concepts like 'realism' which designate perennial modes of representing the world as well as modes characteristic of definite historical movements — for this too the notion of 'family-resemblance' has been found valuable. Here the comparatist has a particularly important part to play. By tracing the history of the words 'romance', 'romantic', 'romantisch' and 'rom-

[10] Wayne Booth, *The Rhetoric of Fiction*, Chicago 1961.
[11] cf. Harry Levin, *The Gates of Horn*, New York 1963, pp. 16-23.
[12] Roy Pascal, *Design and Truth in Autobiography*, London 1960.
[13] In *The Rise of the Novel*, London 1957.

antique' in various countries,[14] he can contribute materially
to the necessary task of distinguishing various kinds of
romanticism; recognizing, with Helmut Hatzfeld, that 'the
characteristics of German Romanticism, namely the serious
belief in the irrational, in poetic intuition and truth, the true
nostalgia for a higher and better life, the belief in meaningful
myth and nature symbolism, are [...] lacking in French
Romanticism',[15] and yet able, with Lilian Furst, to point out
the family likenesses within all this divergence, to show in
what ways the Romantic

creative renewal . . . is adapted to the particular circumstances, to the
indigenous tradition of each land and each literature. But whatever its
special direction, it is inherent in every one of the Romantic
movements as a prime activating force, and as such it forms the flexible
bond that holds together this very diverse family.[16]

Lilian Furst's study gives an account at once of a related
series of literary movements and of a 'period', defined by
Wellek and Warren as 'a time-section dominated by a system
of literary norms, standards and conventions, whose introduction, spread, diversification, integration, and disappearance can be traced'.[17] As this definition implies, such periods
are best studied in relation to the movements that dominate
them, or that exist within them. Period labels like 'Victorian
Age', or *Goethezeit*, are more useful in writing histories of
national literatures than in the international context of
comparative literary studies — though no-one would deny the
heuristic usefulness of larger period labels like 'Middle Ages'.
In all such studies, however, we do well to adopt the
hypothesis put forward by Claudio Guillén: 'A section of
historical time should not be understood as a single entity, a
bloc, a unity, but as a plural number of temporal currents,

[14] cf. Hans Eichner (ed.), *'Romantic' and its Cognates: The European History of
a Word*, Manchester 1972.

[15] Helmut Hatzfeld, 'Comparative literature as a necessary method', in *The
Disciplines of Criticism*, ed. P. Demetz, Th. Greene and L. Nelson, New Haven
1968, p. 89.

[16] Lilian Furst, *Romanticism in Perspective: A Comparative Study of Aspects of the
Romantic movements in England, France and Germany*, ed. cit., p. 286.

[17] Wellek and Warren, *The Theory of Literature*, ed. cit., p. 265.

temporal levels, rhythms or sequences.'[18] A 'current', a 'period', a 'movement' offers no more than a model of description which must be confronted, again and again, with details of the reality whose nature it has been designed to clarify.

In studying concepts like 'Romanticism', 'Realism', 'Naturalism' and 'Symbolism', we may, once again, be moving at different levels of abstraction and generalization; or — to adopt René Wellek's image — within several concentric circles of meaning. Wellek's own discussion of Symbolism furnishes an excellent model of meaningful studies within each of these circles.[19]

First we may study groups of writers who adopted the name in question for their own endeavours. In France there are the *symbolistes*: poets who called, in the late 1880s, for a non-rhetorical poetry and for a break with the tradition of Hugo and the *Parnassiens*. The term *symbolisme* was in fact proposed by Jean Moréas, who started a review called *Le Symbolisme* and published a 'Symbolist' manifesto in *Le Figaro*. The only name beside Moréas's own which is still remembered today among those who regarded themselves as 'symbolists' in the 1880s is that of Gustave Kahn. Other contemporary poets seem to have rejected the label; Verlaine even wrote a little poem beginning 'A bas le symbolisme'.

In the course of time, however, the term *symbolisme* came to describe the broad movement in French poetry from Nerval and Baudelaire to Claudel and Valéry. Here we have stepped into the second of Wellek's four circles. The term now unites poets who differed greatly in outlook, aesthetic theory and literary achievement. This application of the term seems to have begun in the late 1880s (when Mallarmé especially was frequently called a *symboliste*) and in spite of recurring protests, it has held its own right up to the present. In Britain, the term gained currency particularly through Arthur Symons's influential book *The Symbolist Movement in Literature* (1899) and Yeats's essay 'The Symbolism of Poetry' (1900).

Symons and Yeats have already led us into the third of

---

[18] Claudio Guillén, 'Second thoughts on currents and periods', in *The Disciplines of Criticism*, ed. cit., p. 508.

[19] *Discriminations: Further Concepts of Criticism*, New Haven 1970.

Wellek's circles: that in which 'Symbolism' has become a term for a dominant style all over Europe; a style which succeeded nineteenth-century Realism and co-existed with Naturalism. This is where the comparatist's main activities clearly begin. Wellek points out the difficulties — starting with the fact that the term 'Symbolism' (and its linguistic variants) established itself in France, the U.S.A. and Russia, but had much less success in England and Spain and hardly any in Italy and Germany. Yet this is the area of meaning in which the term appears, to Wellek, to be of greatest use: it serves to describe dominant features of post-Realist literature and aesthetic theory, and to indicate resemblances that characterize the literary practice and theory of a number of countries in a given historical period.

'Finally,' Wellek concludes, 'there is the highest abstraction, the [. . .] largest circle: the use of 'symbolism' in all literature, of all ages.' He deprecates this use, though recognizing its existence and occasional justification: 'the term, broken loose from its historical moorings, lacks concrete context and remains merely the name for a phenomenon almost universal in all art.'[20] Yet would not our critical vocabulary be much impoverished if we could not set a universal 'symbolism' (with lower case initial) against a historically limited 'Symbolism'? Is not — by extension and analogy — the term 'realism' as useful for designating a mode of representing the world which is common to many ages as 'Realism' is to denote a dominant style of the nineteenth century? Such terms have a historical and a 'typological' dimension; and the distinction between these has been well and truly drawn by Theodore Ziolkowski in his discussion of Romanticism:

Typological romanticism, as the term implies, refers to an intrinsic attitude toward life that can be found among certain individuals of every era [. . .] Historical Romanticism designates the general outburst of the romantic temper in Europe between roughly 1770 and 1830,[21]

---

[20] ibid., p. 119.

[21] cf. Northrop Frye's insistence on the importance of this historical dimension in *Romanticism Reconsidered: Selected Papers from the English Institute*, New York and London 1963, p. 1: 'Romanticism has a historical centre of gravity, which falls somewhere around the 1790-1830 period. This gets us at once out of

and it includes a whole syndrome of secondary phenomena: a preference for certain literary forms (e.g. the *Märchen*), an interest in 'Romantic' times and places (e.g. the Middle Ages, the Orient), and so forth. When Novalis is called a romantic poet, it is true in both senses: historically and typologically. If someone says that Thomas Mann is a romantic writer, then we infer that this is meant only in the typological sense since the secondary phenomena are not pronounced in his novels.[22]

Both 'typological' and historical romanticism have their place in the 'genealogy of existential thought' which Ziolkowski goes on to trace, with its various responses to a 'basic experience of chaos, doubt, subjectivity and freedom'.[23]

Comparative literary studies may usefully concern themselves with the discriminations and distinctions necessary to justify the appellation 'realistic' to the work of Thomas Mann, say, as well as that of Dickens and Galdós. They may, in the manner of C.S. Lewis, range through world literature in their efforts to discover possible meanings of the word 'realistic', and attempt to arrive at distinctions like those Lewis makes between 'realism of presentation' and 'realism of content':

You can get that of presentation without that of content, as in medieval romance; or that of content without that of presentation, as in French (and some Greek) tragedy; or both together, as in *War and Peace*; or neither, as in the *Orlando Furioso* or *Rasselas* or *Candide*.[24]

They may also trace the evolution of one movement until it passes into, and distinguishes itself from, another (the relation of Realism to Naturalism, for instance, in France and Germany); or study the interrelation of various literary programmes that profess to be opposed to one another.

The progress from Futurism through Dada to Surrealism,

---

the fallacy of timeless characterization, where we say that Romanticism has certain qualities, not found in the age of Pope, of sympathy with nature or what not, only to have some one produce a poem of Propertius and Kalidasa, or, eventually, Pope himself, and demand to know if the same qualities are not there.' That 'timeless characterization' need not be fallacious and that it can usefully supplement historical characterization is demonstrated by Ziolkowski's discussion of 'typological' Romanticism.

[22] Theodore Ziolkowski, *The Novels of Hermann Hesse: A Study in Theme and Structure*, Princeton 1965, pp. 341-2.

[23] ibid., p. 350.

[24] C.S. Lewis, *An Experiment in Criticism*, Cambridge 1961, pp. 59-60.

and thence to the avantgarde movements and manifestoes of
our own day, provides a particularly interesting subject for
the researches just suggested. When Richard Hülsenbeck
isolates, as Dada's special contribution to literature, the
'bruitistic' poem, the 'simultaneistic' poem and the 'static'
poem,[25] it is not difficult to demonstrate, with the help of
Hülsenbeck's own examples, that these 'contributions' can all
be traced back to Italian Futurism (to *bruitismo, simultaneità*
and *parole in libertà*). In each case, however, Dada adds new
devices and changes the import of the old by the anti-
mechanistic, anti-industrial context in which it sets them.
Beyond that, the example I am here suggesting brings home
to us the growing internationalization of literary movements
since the last quarter of the nineteenth century, and the
special place which comparative studies must therefore
occupy in the exploration of modern literature. This point
has been emphatically made by Henry Gifford:

American poets [...] seek to appropriate from sources hitherto
foreign. They close the distances; theirs is a hospitable and a
naturalizing poetry. And the Europeans are not far behind them: Rilke,
possessed by his experience in Russia, then finding in Paris a 'severe and
salutary discipline' which gave him the secret of form; Pasternak, who
felt strong affinities with Rilke; Mandelstam, feeling the spell of Latin
culture and also of the German language; Proust, powerfully attracted
by Ruskin and George Eliot; Yeats, who could not reckon his debt to
Catullus, Verlaine and Mallarmé [...]; Joyce with his wide and
miscellaneous foraging. To understand any one of these writers it is not
enough that you study their own literature. They compel the reader to
look abroad and to live in more than one culture. They demand for
their full appreciation the comparative sense.[26]

There is no doubt, too, that the study of Futurism, Dada and
Surrealism leads its devotees beyond the frontiers not just of
one national literature but also of literature itself. This is true
of most 'period' and 'movement' studies. The very names
with which we try to characterize these frequently suggest
the visual arts (Baroque, Mannerist, Expressionist...).
Romanticism, it has been well said, fulfilled itself in music;

---

[25] Richard Hülsenbeck, *Dada: Eine literarische Dokumentation*, Reinbek 1964,
p. 28.

[26] Henry Gifford, *Comparative Literature*, London 1969, pp. 13-14.

Realism is as important in painting as it is in literature. One need not agree with H.H. Remak's attempt to include 'the comparison of literature with other spheres of human expression' in the very *definition* of 'Comparative Literature' to recognize that scholars ignore such cross-connections and cross-fertilizations at their peril. The light which developments in one art-form can throw on developments in another (what the Germans call, with Oscar Walzel, *wechselseitige Erhellung der Künste*) may be helpful — and no discipline should be so tightly shuttered as to occlude all illumination from outside.

In all the studies discussed in this chapter lurk two dangerous possibilities: the danger of false analogies with the natural sciences (like those on which Brunetière based his genre-theories); and the danger of excessive generalization (like that which bedevilled pioneer studies of the literary Baroque, especially in Germany). Hugh Blair, writing his *Critical Dissertation on the Poems of Ossian* in 1763, already pinpointed these dangers and showed how admirably the English and Scottish empirical tradition is fitted to avoid them:

We can give exact definitions and descriptions of minerals, plants and animals, and can arrange them with precision under the different classes to which they belong, because Nature affords a visible unvarying standard, to which we refer them. But with regard to works of taste and imagination, where Nature has fixed no standard, but leaves scope for beauties of many different kinds, it is absurd to attempt defining and limiting them with the same precision. Criticism, when employed in such attempts, degenerates into trifling questions about words and names only.

This does not mean, of course, that comparative literary studies, or any study of literature, can do without the effort of relating the individual works studied to the historical and social situation within which they were formed; to the literary theories accepted by the age, the generation, the group to which the author belonged; to literary conventions and traditions of which their authors could not but be aware, whatever attitudes towards them they may have chosen to adopt. Literary studies involve periodization — division into time-segments, regarded not as temporal slabs somewhere 'out there', but as hypotheses, 'tools of thought' in E.H. Carr's sense:

> The division of history into periods is not a fact, but a necessary hypothesis or tool of thought, valid in so far as it is illuminating, and dependent for its validity on interpretation.[27]

Ulrich Weisstein, who devotes an illuminating chapter to such concepts as 'epoch', 'period', 'generation', 'movement', 'school' and *cénacle*, speaks of periodization as at once notional and 'real', as *conceptus cum fundamento in re*. This explains, he continues,

> why there can never be definitive, final or immutable definitions. Not only are new facts (the *fundamentum in re*) constantly coming to light, but the standpoint of the observer (*conceptus*) also changes with every generation — beginning with the self-interpretation of periods like the Renaissance or Romanticism. Thus every period, like every work of art, asks to be interpreted in ever new ways from ever changing points of view; every generation demands its own Goethe and its own Baroque.[28]

These are problems every historian of literature has to face; but comparatists must remain aware of an additional complication: what has come to be called 'Romanticism' in one country is neither strictly contemporary nor consistently analogous with what another knows as *Romantik* or *le romantisme*. Subtle discriminations are necessary at every stage. Here, as always in literary study, deduction from theories and models of description must be constantly balanced by induction from the literary works themselves.

One question that frequently arises in comparative 'period' studies is that which asks: how valuable is it to juxtapose literary phenomena very disparate in nature and without clearly discernible historical contact? What insights can be derived from a comparison of, for instance, the great flowering of literature in sixteenth- and seventeenth-century England with that in seventeenth-century France? An answer may be found in the justly celebrated passage from Lytton Strachey's *Landmarks in French Literature* (first published in

[27] E.H. Carr, *What is History?*, London 1961, Chapter 3.

[28] Ulrich Weisstein, *Einführung in die Vergleichende Literaturwissenschaft*, ed. cit., p. 127.

1912) which sets out to compare Shakespeare and Racine. Strachey begins by sketching the tradition within which each of these masters must be seen and then goes on to compare, in greater detail, a characteristic play by Racine — *Bérénice* — with one by Shakespeare — *Antony and Cleopatra*. The choice of these plays, Strachey is careful to point out, is not arbitrary:

The two dramas, while diametrically opposed in treatment, yet offer some curious parallels in the subjects with which they deal. Both are concerned with a pair of lovers placed in the highest position of splendour and power; in both the tragedy comes about through a fatal discordance between the claims of love and the world; in both the action passes in the age of Roman greatness, and vast imperial issues are intertwined with individual destinies.[29]

The comparison that follows stresses differences rather than resemblances, in order to bring out the special flavour of Racine, so strange to tastes formed by Shakespeare; in order to increase understanding and enlarge sympathy.

It behoves an Englishman, before he condemns or despises a foreign writer, to practise some humility and do his best to understand the point of view from which that writer is regarded by his own compatriots. No doubt, in the case of Racine, this is a particularly difficult matter. There are genuine national antipathies to be got over — real differences in habits of thought and taste. But this very difficulty, when it is once surmounted, will make the gain the greater. For it will be a gain, not only in the appreciation of one additional artist, but in the appreciation of a new *kind* of artist; it will open up a whole undiscovered country in the continent of art.[30]

The work so well begun by Strachey is carried on by Martin Turnell in the opening chapter of *The Classical Moment*.[31] Here the differences between Shakespeare's drama and Racine's, between seventeenth-century English and seventeenth-century French literature, are traced to their historical and social determinants: to divergent social and literary developments leading to divergent institutions, con-

[29] Lytton Strachey, *Landmarks in French Literature*, London 1948, p. 57.

[30] Strachey, op. cit., pp. 53-4.

[31] Martin Turnell, *The Classical Moment: Studies of Corneille, Molière and Racine*, London 1947.

ventions and climates of thought; to the different kinds of audience addressed by the two dramatists, with their differing expectations and notions of decorum. The result, for the critical reader,[32] is a new and better understanding of both — the kind of understanding Herder had tried to promote when he compared, in his essay on Shakespeare published in 1773, Elizabethan and ancient Greek traditions of drama; the kind of understanding A.W. Schlegel had so sadly lacked when, in his celebrated and influential *Lectures on Dramatic Art and Literature* (first delivered at Vienna in 1808), he preceded his loving exegesis of Shakespeare with jaundiced remarks on the French theatre in the age of Corneille, Racine and Molière. An understanding of widely divergent literary phenomena in their historical and social setting, and an ability to enlarge his readers' literary sympathies through judicious juxtaposition and exegesis, would seem to be the most valuable gifts the comparatist can bring to his arduous but rewarding task.

---

[32] Such a reader would almost certainly want to dissent from Martin Turnell's view that Milton 'wrote a "Christian epic" which betrays in every line his utter disbelief in the fundamental tenets of the Christian system' (op. cit., p. 6).

8.
Structure and Ideas

The comparative study of literary periods and movements leads, inevitably, to that of devices and structures. When talking of the links between Italian Futurism and the Dadaists of Zurich, we could not but mention attempts to achieve *simultaneità, Gleichzeitigkeit,* simultaneity: attempts made again and again, in different ways, to confound Lessing's famous distinction between literature as the art of succession and the visual arts as those of juxtaposition, between literature's movement in time and the visual arts' stasis in space. More and more writers have tried, especially since the beginning of the present century, to overcome the 'succession' of literary events and render the 'simultaneity', the co-presence of many different impressions and thoughts at one of the same moment, which is so strongly impressed on us by modern city life. From the Futurists until Bernard Heidsieck in our own day we have had attempts to produce the *poème simultané* in which several voices, or one voice mechanically reproduced several times and then super-imposed, spoke and chanted together. From Apollinaire to the 'Concrete' poets we have seen attempts to revive *technopaignia,* poem-pictures in which words are so disposed on the page that they make a meaningful pattern which can be taken in at a glance; and more significantly, there have been many attempts by novelists, including the greatest, to suggest the co-existence in the mind of past and present, the mingling of memory, sensation and desire, and the many different personalities that may be co-present within one biological entity. The comparative study of devices that produce effects of 'simultaneity' leads from the lunatic fringes to the very centre of modern literature: to Proust's 'binocular' and 'stereoscopic' effects; to Joyce's prefigurations and portmanteau-words; to Thomas Mann's use of *leitmotif* in *Buddenbrooks*, myth in the *Joseph* novels and double time-perspective in *Dr. Faustus*; and to the many experiments with multiple perspective which we find in Gide, Huxley, Dos Passos and Faulkner.

The examples just suggested are part of that *Rhetoric of Fiction* which in our time can best be studied on an international, comparative basis: studies, above all, in narrational 'voice' and point of view, in different ways of 'interiorizing' fiction through stream-of-consciousness techniques (from Garshin's *Four Days* to Dujardin's *The Laurels Are Cut Down* and Schnitzler's *Lieutenant Gustl*) or through devices variously termed 'free indirect discourse', *style indirect libre* and *erlebte Rede* (from Jane Austen to Flaubert to Uwe Johnson).

It often happens that observations made by writers in one language when they attempt to clarify their own practice turn out to be helpful in clarifying the practice of writers in another. Reinhold Grimm has therefore been able to use Gottfried Benn's desription of his 'phenotype novel' — in form like the segments of an orange, all tending towards a centre — to explain the structure of Huysmans's *Against Nature* [*A Rebours*] and Valéry's *Monsieur Teste*;[1] Theodore Ziolkowski, in a notable essay, has discussed the modern German novel in the light of Joyce's account of 'epiphanies' in *Stephen Hero*;[2] and Henry James's critical terms ('registers' and 'centres', 'scenes' and 'pictures') have shown themselves adequate to the description of narrative structures in many languages. Conversely, the study of a French phenomenon like the *nouveau roman* gains much from a European perspective and comparative treatment: Robbe-Grillet's attempts, for instance, to render the 'thinginess' of things, apart from their human and symbolic aspect, may well be seen in the context of a European, indeed world-wide,

---

[1] Reinhold Grimm, *Strukturen: Essays zur deutschen Literatur*, Göttingen 1963, p. 88.

[2] Theodore Ziolkowski, 'James Joyces Epiphanie und die Überwindung der empirischen Welt in der modernen deutschen Prosa', *Deutsche Vierteljahrsschrift für Literaturwissenschaft und Geistesgeschichte* XXXV (1961).

feeling of alienation and 'commodity fetishism'. They may also suggest, in a world-wide perspective, the limits within which literature can present objects apart from their symbolic and human associations: as Bruce Morrissette and Roland Barthes have shown, the Balzacian and Dickensian reflections of man in the things that surround him have not been as radically eliminated from Robbe-Grillet's novels as his theoretical writings might lead one to suppose.

Comparative study of the use of symbols in literature — into which study of the *nouveau roman* must enter — is a fruitful field that could bear further cultivation, even though some of the work done has been so unimaginative that someone has recently proposed a Society for the Protection of Symbols from Literary Critics. A model of how this kind of study can be meaningful, across genres as well as across languages and national frontiers, is Walter Sokel's confrontation of the way Flaubert and Strindberg introduce the figure of a beggar into their work.

Sokel begins by analysing the 'three-dimensional reality' of the blind, disfigured beggar introduced at various points of *Madame Bovary*: he is evoked as an individual, well-rounded and credible, to whom other individuals in the novel react in characteristic ways. At the same time, however, the beggar appears at moments in which he can clearly stand, for the reader, in a functional relationship to Emma Bovary's inner life. His appearances foreshadow, parallel and underline the main idea of the work and the essence of the heroine's existence. Character has become symbol; a character is used like a metaphor. Just as a metaphor can convey and underline the emotional meaning of a passage, so the beggar in Flaubert's novel reinforces the emotional effect of the whole novel. His appearances act like musical variations of a theme. At the same time, however, the beggar becomes expressive of Emma Bovary's inner state.

In the very work which represents the crowning achievement of nineteenth-century Realism, Flaubert anticipates a device essential to Expressionism. He expresses the main character's repressed feeling or repressed awareness by embodying them in another character; this symbolic character becomes then the objective correlative for inner states which the main character has concealed from himself. He makes what is unknown to the character, but significant about him and hidden within him, visible to the reader without directly informing him as traditional narrative was wont to do.[3]

It is this last function which becomes dominant in the beggar who appears in Strindberg's *To Damascus* (1898). That figure, Sokel shows, is not credible, and not meant to be credible, as an actual person:

He is entirely what Flaubert's beggar is partially — an aspect of the main character and an adumbration of his fate. He is the degradation which the haughty protagonist dreads and the resignation which he has not yet learned. He is the embodiment of the hero's repressed and unrealized emotions and thoughts, and the personification of a possibility of existence toward which the hero must move.[4]

and again:

In this case [. . .] the symbol points beyond itself, to be sure; however, it points not outward to a world, a cosmos, but inward, back to the work of which it forms a part. The character becomes somewhat similar to a musical note which receives its meaning not by representing anything objective in the external world, but solely by functioning in a self-enclosed, artificial world, a composition.[5]

Through his detailed analysis of two ways of using a character as a symbol, Sokel has been able to show not only the difference between two major European writers but also one of the ways in which Realism turned into Expressionism — a transformation of whose social background and significance he shows himself well aware.

In his discussion of the two 'beggar' figures Sokel stresses their importance for the *structure* of the work in which they occur; and this may serve as a welcome reminder that comparative studies, like all literary studies, must ultimately be concerned with wholes, with works which form a 'system' in the sense that every detail has its place and function in a total structure. For simpler structures, like folk-tales, convincing typologies can be and have been suggested: typologies

---

[3] W.H. Sokel, *The Writer in Extremis: Expressionism in Twentieth-century German Literature*, Stanford 1969, p. 33.

[4] op. cit., p. 35.

[5] op. cit., p. 34.

which must all take account of the pioneering work of Vladimir Propp.[6] Analysing a corpus of a hundred tales, Propp has suggested an ever-recurring scheme within the surface variety of different plots: a 'deep structure' based on the function of different actions or motifs. The latter Propp designates by such labels as 'evil deed', 'struggle (against the evil-doer)', 'victory (over the evil-doer)': each of these subsumes, not a single event, but a class of events, and each class has its specific function and place in the plot of the whole tale. The 'evil deed', for instance, sets the events in motion, and so makes way for the next functional unit in the plot sequence. Propp's analysis seeks to demonstrate that under their enormous surface variety Russian folk-tales conceal the same basic structure, even though not all of them exhibit every one of the functional units he has isolated: if one of these is missing, the others still appear in unaltered sequence. In his stimulating paper on 'Generative grammar and the theory of literature' (read to the XIth International Congress of Linguists at Bucharest in 1967), Morton Bloomfield has applied Propp's methods to Chaucer's *Man of Law's Tale* and the seventh story of the second day of Boccaccio's *Decameron*. Bloomfield shows that two works which on the surface tell quite different stories, with a moral content the very opposite of each other, may yet have identical structures:

An attractive woman is sent to a foreign country where she is to marry an unknown man of high station or degree. The marriage is prevented (through a storm or hostile human beings). The heroine has a series of adventures, which include encounters with Moslems and Christians, long journeys, shipwrecks, murders, language problems and above all designs on her virtue (which are either accepted or rejected). At last she reaches and marries the man intended for her husband.

Within this over-all scheme, the heroine may be either sinful or virtuous, a liar or truthful: Boccaccio's Alatiel is the sinful reverse of Chaucer's virtuous Constance. Each story is the

---

[6] Vladimir Propp, *Morphology of the Folk-tale*, Baltimore 1958. The original Russian version was published in Leningrad in 1928. Propp's distinction between a deep structure of 'plot' and a surface structure of 'story' has gained wide acceptance; the details of his interpretation have, however, been frequently challenged. cf. Claude Brémond, 'Le Message naratif', *Communications* IV (1964), pp. 4-32.

antithesis of the other while the scheme of the story remains the same. In fact each story, without reference to the other, suggests something of its counterpart: the innocence of Constance has a sexual suggestiveness and allure, and within Alatiel's sinful yielding in situations not of her own making there is something of innocence. It should go without saying that recognition of such basic patterns must go hand in hand with recognition of the original way in which Chaucer and Boccaccio have filled them out — but disciples of Propp do not always resist the temptation to which, according to J.R.R. Tolkien, students of folklore tend to succumb when dealing with epics and fairy-tales:

They are inclined to say that any two stories that are built around the same folk-lore motive, or are made up of a generally similar combination of such motives, are 'the same stories'. We read that *Beowulf* is only a version of *Dat Erdmänneken*'; that 'The Black Bull of Norroway* is *Beauty and the Beast*', or 'is the same story as *Eros and Psyche*'; and the Norse *Mastermaid* (or the Gaelic *Battle of the Birds* and its many congeners and variants) is 'the same story as the Greek tale of Jason and Medea'.[7]

Even when we have learnt, from Propp, Bloomfield and Todorov,[8] to look for the 'deep structures' discernible in works of literature no less than in languages, we shall do well to heed Tolkien's warning not to neglect 'the colouring, the atmosphere, the unclassifiable individual details of a story'; not to neglect, either, 'the general purport that informs with life the undissected bones of the plot' — all that makes Shakespeare's *King Lear* 'different from Layamon's story in his *Brut*'.[9]

Albert Cook has attempted an over-all view, on a comparative basis, of plot-types more complicated than those of Propp's folk-tales and Bloomfield's *fabliaux* and *novelle*. One of the distinctions he has proposed is that between plots of 'design' and plots of 'process':[10]

---

[7] J.R.R. Tolkien, 'On fairy-stories', in *Tree and Leaf*, London 1964, p. 22.

[8] See especially Tzvetan Todorov's *Grammaire du Décaméron*, The Hague 1971.

[9] Tolkien, op. cit., p. 23.

[10] Albert Cook, *The Meaning of Fiction*, Detroit 1960.

We can distinguish between plots whose causality seems contained in their beginning and plots whose causality generates itself anew through the middle and the end in such a way that by the end we are on totally unexpected ground. *Oedipus Rex* has a plot of the first kind; the drama advances by trying to reveal/conceal the implications of an action given but not understood at the very beginning [. . .] However large the scale of the action in plots of [this] first type, the end is causally implied in the beginning; the *Agamemnon* demands the middle of the *Choephorae*, the resolution of the *Eumenides* [. . .] In plots of the second type, those whose causality generates anew through the middle and the end, we move as we read into ground both unknown and unexpected. Qualitative change, metamorphosis, is constantly taking place. After twelve years and over a thousand pages Pierre in *War and Peace* has attained a staunch wisdom and genial penetration inconceivable for the bumbling egoist of the novel's beginning . . .[11]

As Cook's examples suggest, such plot-types may correspond to genres — one tends to find plots of design in the drama, plots of process in the novel; but it is not unusual to find these genre distinctions transcended, particularly in more recent literature. Other of Cook's classifications deserve testing and elaborating: his description of a 'reaction' plot, for instance, exemplified by *Don Quixote*, Gogol's *Dead Souls* and Melville's *The Confidence Man*; a type of plot in which the central character moves through a world whose denizens reveal what is in them by their differing reaction, their unique responses, to the situations he creates — reactions 'to what is basically the same situation, the same person, for each'.[12]

As in the differentiation of literary movements and styles, from Baroque to Surrealism, so in the classification of different literary structures critics have learnt a great deal from historians of the visual arts. Heinrich Wölfflin's distinction, for instance, between 'closed' and 'open' forms has been applied, with some success, to types of drama. In a subtly argued and carefully documented study,[13] Volker Klotz has distinguished a 'closed' form whose ideal type is approached by Racine from an 'open' form whose ideal type is approached by Georg Büchner; he has been able to show how tendencies in the direction of the 'closed' or 'open' form

[11] op. cit., pp. 16-17.
[12] op. cit., p. 19.

have predominated in certain societies and certain ages, and he has done so without losing sight either of counter-currents and individual variations or of the great synthesis of both forms in the work of Shakespeare. Nor is it only the visual arts that can suggest useful analogies: music, too, has been raided, by authors no less than critics, for a meaningful critical vocabulary. Alfred Döblin, for instance, has contrasted his own 'homophonic' method of construction with a 'polyphonic' method like that of Dos Passos, at the centre of whose work are not one but many leading figures and foci of consciousness. Dos Passos obtains broad effects by following various protagonists along their different courses through the city and through the years; Döblin's *Berlin Alexanderplatz* concentrates, in the main, on the progress of one central figure, Franz Biberkopf, and his relation to the many forces that act upon him in the German capital.[14]

Our understanding of lyric poetry has also benefited by the concern comparatists have shown, in recent years, with types of over-all design and over-all structure. The nature of modern poetry, for instance, has been greatly illuminated by Hugo Friedrich's demonstration, in his study of structural principles in the modern lyric,[15] of the way in which the course of the European lyric has been constantly affected, in the twentieth century, by the recollection or independent rediscovery of the procedures of Rimbaud and Mallarmé. The stylistic traits discussed by Friedrich — dissonantic tension, aggressive dynamism, disorientation, deliberate incoherence, cult of the fragment, reversability, 'estrangement', parataxis etc. — have sharpened discussion of all recent poetry and allowed easier definition of such originality as its practitioners may be said to exhibit. An additional question it has raised, in a European context, is why most of Friedrich's categories should be 'negative' or 'antagonistic': a question which has a clear bearing on the self-image, the function and the status of poets in modern society. Friedrich's analyses,

---

[13] Volker Klotz, *Geschlossene und offene Form im Drama*, München 1960.

[14] For another use of the terms 'homophonic' and 'polyphonic' in criticism of the novel, see M.M. Bakhtin, *Problemy tvorchestva Dostoevskogo*, Leningrad 1929.

[15] Hugo Friedrich, *Die Struktur der modernen Lyrik*, Hamburg 1956.

and the questions they raised, are usefully supplemented by Elizabeth Sewell,[16] and by Iris Murdoch in her book on Sartre:

> To lose the discursive 'thingy' nature of one's vision and yet to feel the necessity of utterance is to experience a breakdown of language which may be met in either of two extreme ways. The poet may accept and even intensify his sense of the chaotic interpenetration of reality and attempt to make his language into the perfect expression of this over-rich world. To do this is to weaken the referential character of language by overloading it. On the other hand, the poet may attempt to draw language out of the ineffable flux altogether, and to erect it into a pure and non-referential structure on its own. The former reaction was that of Rimbaud, the latter that of Mallarmé.[17]

A study of the problems faced by Baudelaire, Rimbaud and Mallarmé, and the way they tackled them, would seem to be an indispensible precondition of all studies of modern European poetry.

Here once again, as so often, the historical study of literary phenomena shades over into history of ideas; and it is surely significant, in this connection, that Harvard University chose to inaugurate its series of *Studies in Comparative Literature* with a work in which a philosopher looked at three of the masterpieces of Western literature in order to see how far these were affected by, and how far they reflected, the philosophical spirit of their times. The philosopher was George Santayana; the three works were Lucretius's *De rerum natura*, Dante's *Divine Comedy* and Goethe's *Faust*. Santayana treats each of these works as representative of a type of imagination and a type of philosophy characteristic of their time, and then goes on to attempt a comparison between them:

> Goethe, in his *Faust*, presents experience in its immediacy, variety and apparent groundlessness; and [. . .] he presents it as an episode, before and after which other episodes, differing from it more and more as you recede, may be conceived to come. There is no possible totality in this, for there is no known ground. Turn to Lucretius, and the difference is striking. Lucretius is the poet of substance. The ground is what he sees everywhere; and by seeing the ground, he sees also the possible

---

[16] Elizabeth Sewell, *The Structure of Poetry*, London 1951.

[17] Iris Murdoch, *Sartre: Romantic Rationalist*, Cambridge 1953, p. 27.

products of it. Experience appears in Lucretius, not as each man comes upon it in his own person, but as the scientific observer views it from without. Experience for him is a natural, inevitable, monotonous round of feelings, involved in the operations of nature. The ground and the limits of experience have become evident together.

In Dante, on the other hand, we have a view of experience also in its totality, also from above and, in a sense, from outside; but the external point of reference is moral, not physical, and what interests the poet is what experience is best [. . .] Here, then, are our three poets and their messages: Goethe, with human life in its immediacy, treated romantically; Lucretius, with a vision of nature and of the limits of human life; Dante, with spiritual mastery of that life, and a perfect knowledge of good and evil.

These few sentences from the conclusion of his book cannot adequately convey Santayana's packed and complex argument; but they should suffice to suggest how misleading his generalizations are. They fail signally to do justice to the complexity of Goethe, who saw 'the ground' as clearly as Lucretius, though it was a different ground, governed by different laws, laws of metamorphosis and 'heightening'; who also had visions of good and evil no less clear than those of Dante, though different in kind.

The failure of Santayana's pioneer attempt should not, however, blind us to the importance of linking the study of literature with that of the history of ideas. Here the writings of A.O. Lovejoy — particularly *The Great Chain of Being* and *Essays in the History of Ideas*[18] — can still prove stimulating and helpful. Lovejoy concentrates attention on 'unit-ideas', defined as

types of categories, thoughts concerning particular aspects of common experience, implicit or explicit presuppositions, sacred formulas and catchwords, specific philosophical theorems, or the larger hypotheses, generalizations or methodological assumptions of various sciences — which have long life-histories of their own, are to be found at work in the most various regions of the history of human thinking and feeling, and upon which the intellectual and affective reactions of men — individuals and masses — have been highly diverse.[19]

---

[18] A.O. Lovejoy, *The Great Chain of Being: A Study in the History of Ideas*, Cambridge, Mass., 1936, and *Essays in the History of Ideas*, Baltimore 1948.

[19] *Essays in the History of Ideas*, ed. cit., p. 9.

These ideas Lovejoy tracks down in many provinces of
thought and several periods of history, paying due attention
to semantic transitions and confusions, to internal tensions
and waverings in the mind of individual writers; tensions and
waverings which are due to 'conflicting ideas or incongruous
propensities of taste'.[20] Most important of all: Lovejoy does
not allow the similarities he detects between the philosophers, scientists and poets he has studied to deflect our
appreciation of their individuality. He endorses, for instance,
much that S.F. Gingerich has to say about Coleridge's debt to
Kant — but he rightly demurs when Gingerich goes on to see
in 'Dejection: An Ode' 'the fullest expression to be found in
[Coleridge's] poetry of the transcendental principle'.

> I see them all, so excellently fair,
> I see, not feel, how beautiful they are.

This inability to respond emotionally to the spectacle of nature was,
obviously, not the consequence of a reading of the *Kritik der reinen
Vernunft*; the generalization which Coleridge bases upon this experience was not to be found in that work, which has nothing to say about
the fact of empirical psychology that is dwelt upon in the poem; 'joy'
was *not* one of the *a priori* categories of Kant; and there is not even a
formal parallel between Coleridge's psychological observation and
Kant's metaphysical theorem, since 'the mind' which Kant makes the
source of the *a priori* percepts (space and time) and the categories is
the generic mind, identical in all men and unmodified by circumstances,
while Coleridge is insisting upon the *differences* between the aesthetic
reactions of individual minds — and specifically, of his own mind (at
the moment) and Wordsworth's — and even of the same mind in
different moods.
   There is in the Ode, it is true, the poetic intimation of an aesthetic
theory; and this is in accord with the Kantian aesthetics in so far as it
admits that there may be an intellectual recognition that an object is
abstractly 'beautiful', without emotion: 'I see, not feel, how beautiful
they are.' But Kant had scornfully (and characteristically) declared that
any 'taste that requires an added element of *emotion* and *charm* for its
delight, not to speak of adopting this as the measure of its approval, has
not yet emerged from barbarism'; whereas the burden of Coleridge's
poem is the emptiness of this unemotionalized judgment, the indispensa-
bility, for any genuine aesthetic experience, of the non-intellectual and
non-univeral element which Kant had so loftily dismissed.[21]

---

[20] op. cit., pp. xii-xiv.
[21] op. cit., pp. 261-2.

Through such discriminations Lovejoy does justice at once to Coleridge's debt to German idealist philosophy and to his individuality as man and poet.

In recent years the presuppositions of Lovejoy's 'history of ideas' have been challenged by Michel Foucault, whose *Words and Things* and *The Archaeology of Knowledge*[22] represent sustained attempts to replace the 'history' of thought by its 'archaeology': not to seek antecedents for 'unit-ideas', but rather to analyse the structural similarities that exist, in a given historical period, between different sciences and arts — between, for instance, the philology, the biology and the economic structure of nineteenth-century Europe. Foucault's studies may serve to make us more aware of relationships ignored in diachronic accounts of a single field of thought; they may help us to see the relevance of philosophical, ethical, psychological, economic and scientific ideas to the very structure and texture of works of literature. But in comparative literary studies, as in linguistics, there will always be a need for diachronic studies to supplement synchronic ones. No structuralist critique has, as yet, invalidated works like Lovejoy's *The Great Chain of Being* or E.M.W. Tillyard's *The Elizabethan World Picture*,[23] whose demonstration of the way in which the argument of Shakespeare's plays, their structure and their imagery relate to patterns of thought inherited from the European Middle Ages remains valid. Their work constitutes an encouragement to similar investigation of more recent literature and thought. It is useful and illuminating to study the relations that exist between Bergson's notions of time and 'stream of conscious-ness' techniques, between the ideas of Freud and Jung and Surrealist literary practices, between Clark Maxwell's physics and the novels of Max Frisch, between scientific 'comple-mentarity' theories and the literary experiments of our own day. How little this is simply a matter of 'influence', and how necessary it is to see literature in the context of the other arts as well as of the history of philosophical and scientific thought, may be seen from a representative passage in a

[22] Michel Foucault. *Les Mots et les choses*, Paris 1966, and *L'Archéologie du savoir*, Paris 1969.

[23] E.M.W. Tillyard, *The Elizabethan World Picture*, London 1943.

recent book which relates modern literary attitudes and practices to the thought of Ernst Mach.

Mach's impressionistic philosophy postulated a world that was neither mental nor material, subjective nor objective, but rather composed of neutral elements called sensations (*Empfindungen*). In Mach's view all previous dualisms and dialectics of German metaphysics [. . .] dissolve (as they do in the empiricist philosophy of Hume, an avowed forerunner of Mach's) into a monistic system of glittering sensations. Much as in the world of Pissarro, Monet and Seurat, the subject-object plane dissolves into a sea of many-coloured points, so much so that the personality itself becomes nothing more than a sum of atomistic, 'objective' sensations without an organizing centre [. . .] The parallel between Mach's thought and Hofmannsthal's poetry should be clear: the emphasis on life as a series of impressions or sensations, the illusory quality of the self, and the resultant dependency upon sheer memory for the cult of personality are common to both writers.[24]

What begins as an account of a single Austrian novel widens inevitably into a consideration of the history of European philosophy between Hume and Wittgenstein, and of the Impressionist revolution in the visual arts.

At almost every point, then, comparative literary studies lead over into, or presuppose, studies in cultural history and history of ideas. Philosophical movements, new psychologies, shifts in an overall world view often lead to the rediscovery, reinterpretation or revaluation of great literary figures of other cultures and climes. Prominent recent examples include the discovery of Kleist and Büchner by the French existentialists, or (a little further back) that of the German Romantics, and of the poetry of Hölderlin's madness, by the Surrealists. For neither literature nor ideas operate in a vacuum. They are produced by and for men: by gifted individuals who cannot but respond to the nature of the world, the kind of society, within which they live, and to the expectations of those for whom they write. They are received by men: by individual hearers, readers, spectators at a definite historical moment, who have problems and interests which are not confined to literature and philosophical systems but which may be reflected in, and may be affected by, both. In comparing the organization of different literary

---

[24] D.H. Miles, *Hofmannsthal's Novel* Andreas: *Memory and Self*, Princeton 1972, pp. 38-9.

works at all levels, from metrical and grammatical forms to the choice and organization of different subjects and themes, we must never lose sight of these wider connections — even if we are not prepared to follow Lucien Goldmann, and other Structuralist and Marxist critics, in seeking precise 'structural homologies'[25] between the composition and thought of a given social group and the works of literature produced in its midst. We must beware, at the same time, of obliterating the distinction between literature and philosophy:

In literature ideas are no longer quite ideas; they become a part of a differently realized world of experience, in which ideas are related to linguistic enactments and to speakers, and in which the force of language is never wholly rational — as Yeats suggested, when he asked to be guarded from 'those thoughts Men think in the mind alone'.[26]

The work of the comparatist, like that of every literary scholar, must be directed at once inwards, towards the heterocosm of the literary work, and outwards, towards the world in which authors and their readers live, a world whose concern with literature is not exclusive.

---

[25] For a cogent exposition and critique of the 'homology' concept Goldmann used in *Le Dieu caché* and *Pour une sociologie du roman*, see Robert Escarpit (ed.), *Le Littéraire et le social: Eléments pour une sociologie de la littérature*, Paris 1970, pp. 16-17, 50, 61, 64 and 121; and Peter Demetz: 'Wandlungen der marxistischen Literaturkritik: Hans Mayer, Ernst Fischer, Lucien Goldmann', in *Der Dichter und seine Zeit: Politik im Spiegel der Literatur* (Drittes Amherster Kolloquium zur modernen deutschen Literatur), Heidelberg 1970, pp. 24-31.

[26] Malcolm Bradbury, *The Social Context of Modern English Literature*, Oxford 1971, p. 256.

9.
'Placing'

No one who has ever read Erich Auerbach's *Mimesis* will forget its confrontation, in the opening chapter, of a passage from the nineteenth book of the *Odyssey* with one from Chapter 22 of *Genesis*. In lovingly detailed exegesis Homer's narrative of the way Euryclea recognized the returning Ulysses by his scar, and the Elohist's narrative of Abraham's journey to sacrifice Isaac, are held against one another, and allowed to illuminate each other's narrative virtues and limitations.

On the one hand, externalized, uniformly illuminated phenomena, at a definite time and a definite place, connected together without lacunae in a perpetual foreground; thoughts and feeling completely expressed; events taking place in leisurely fashion and with very little of suspense. On the other hand, the externalization of only so much of the phenomena as is necessary for the purpose of the narrative, all else left in obscurity; the decisive points of the narrative alone are emphasized, what lies between is non-existent; time and place are indefined and call for interpretation; thoughts and feeling remain unexpressed, are only suggested by the silence and the fragmentary speeches; the whole, permeated with the most unrelieved suspense and directed towards a single goal (and to that extent far more of a unity), remains mysterious and 'fraught with background'.[1]

Many of the conclusions Auerbach sought to draw from his confrontation of these two passages may be challenged. Is it really two 'epic' styles he is contrasting here — or should the style of the Biblical passage be called 'dramatic'? Is it fair to generalize about Greek literature from the undoubtedly true contention that in the Biblical narrative 'humiliation and

---

[1] Erich Auerbach, *Mimesis: The Representation of Reality in Western Literature*, translated by Willard Trask, New York 1957, p. 9.

elevation go far deeper and far higher than in Homer', without mentioning Oedipus, or Antigone, or Electra? Does not Hesiod's *Works and Days*, with its serious presentation, in an epic style, of the wretched life of a Boeotian farmer, belie Auerbach's claim that 'everything commonly realistic, everything pertaining to everyday life, must not be treated on any level except the comic, which admits no problematic probing'?[2] It is possible to raise all these questions, and many more, without detracting from Auerbach's achievement, here and throughout *Mimesis*, in so choosing, and so analysing, his passages from many works in many languages that they 'place' one another. We see more in the Biblical passage because it has been held against a passage from the *Odyssey*; we see more in the *Odyssey* because it has been held against the Bible; we see more in both because each is first looked at in its own context, against its own traditions, on its own ground. Auerbach's careful analysis, with its constant reference to texts which are, for the most part, actually before us, shows up comparison across linguistic frontiers as a powerful method of distinguishing different styles, and common or different traditions, within world literature — even if our own interpretation, at times, goes counter to Auerbach's, even if our own notion of the way 'representation' and 'reality' are related is more differentiated than his.

By 'placing', then, I mean the mutual illumination of several texts, or series of texts, considered side by side; the greater understanding we derive from juxtaposing a number of (frequently very different) works, authors and literary traditions. This may take many forms besides those already illustrated in earlier chapters. At its simplest, it may be a way of bringing out more clearly the manner in which one author habitually structures his work, by contrasting it with another:

Unlike Balzac, Dostoevsky tends to avoid bald exposition whenever possible; instead of a preliminary scene setting, he begins with action, and the reality of the scene is built in passing, by a host of details called forth in the order of their relevance to what is going on. The setting is a function of the action [. . .][3]

---

[2] ibid., p. 27.

[3] Donald Fanger, *Dostoevsky and Romantic Realism*, ed. cit., p. 192.

More complex is the kind of 'explanatory' placing with which James J.Y. Liu has put all Western readers in his debt: the way he illustrates the unfamiliar material from Chinese literature included in *The Chinese Knight Errant*[4] by comparisons and contrasts with the chivalric literature and ideals of medieval Europe. Or, in another mode, one might point to Northrop Frye's demonstration of the way in which the words 'romantic' and 'realistic' may be used as

> relative or comparative terms: they illustrate tendencies in fiction, and cannot be used as simply descriptive adjectives with any sort of exactness. If we take the sequence *De Raptu Proserpinae, The Man of Law's Tale, Much Ado About Nothing, Pride and Prejudice, An American Tragedy*, it is clear that each work is 'romantic' compared to its successors and 'realistic' compared to its predecessors.[5]

The works Frye lists define one another's place on a scale whose one end he labels 'romantic' while the other is 'realistic'.

Yet another mode of literary 'placing' may be illustrated from Matthew Arnold's essay 'Last Words on Translating Homer' (1862). In an earlier work, Arnold had enumerated the qualities of Homer's style which no translator should be prepared to sacrifice, and had included among these 'that Homer did not rise and sink with his subject, was never to be called prosaic or low'.[6] This called forth protests that parts of the *Iliad* were, in fact, pitched lower than others. 'But', Arnold now answers,

> 'I never denied that a *subject* must rise and sink, that it must have its elevated and its level regions; all I deny is, that a poet can be said to rise and sink when all that he, as a poet, can do, is perfectly well done'. A poet may sink by being 'falsely grand' in a place where his subject calls for simplicity, as well as by being 'low'.
> A passage of the simplest narrative is quoted to me from Homer:—

ὄτρυνεν δὲ ἕκαστον ἐποιχόμενος ἐπέεσσι,
Μέσθλην τε Γλαῦκόν τε Μέδοντά τε Θερσίλοχόν τε . . .[7]

---

[4] James J.Y. Liu, *The Chinese Knight Errant*, London 1967.

[5] Northrop Frye, *Anatomy of Criticism*, loc. cit., p. 49.

[6] Matthew Arnold, *On Translating Homer: Three Lectures*, 1861.

[7] 'To rouse their spirit he went up and spoke to each of them in turn: to Mesthles and Glaucus; to Medon and Thersilochus . . .' *Iliad* XVII, 215-16 — E.V. Rieu's translation.

and I am asked, whether Homer does not sink *there*; whether he '*can have intended such lines as those for poetry?*' My answer is: Those lines are very good poetry indeed, poetry of the best class, *in that place*. But when Wordsworth, having to narrate a very plain matter, tries *not* to sink in narrating it, tries, in short, to be what is falsely called poetical, he does sink, although he sinks by being pompous, not by being low.

> Onward we drove beneath the Castle; caught
> While crossing Magdalen Bridge, a glimpse of Cam,
> And at the Hoop alighted, famous inn.

The last line shows excellently how a poet may sink with his subject by resolving not to sink with it. A page or two father on, the subject rises to grandeur, and then Wordsworth is nobly worthy of it:

> The antechapel, where the statue stood
> Of Newton with his prism and silent face,
> The marble index of a mind for ever
> Voyaging through strange seas of thought, alone.

But the supreme poet is he who is thoroughly sound and poetical, alike when this subject is grand, and when it is plain: with him the subject may sink, but never the poet.[8]

This illuminates the nature of the sustained 'Grand Style', as Arnold had learnt to recognize it in Homer, by judicious quotation from a work in English; a work which achieves a grandeur at least equal to Homer's in some parts but fails, as a whole, to achieve Homer's poise. It 'places' Homer, and it 'places' Wordsworth.

In the example from Matthew Arnold we are asked — as we are not in those from Auerbach and Frye — to distinguish differences in value as well as differences in style: to see a 'good' grand style thrown into relief by a 'bad' one. Such aesthetic judgments often shade, in Arnold's criticism, into moral judgement. His celebrated essay on *Anna Karenina*, for instance, opposes Tolstoy to Flaubert in a way wholly characteristic of a critic who saw in literature a 'criticism of life':

Madame Bovary [. . .] is a work of *petrified feeling*; over it hangs an atmosphere of bitterness, irony, impotence; not a personage in the

---

[8] Matthew Arnold, *Essays Literary and Critical*, Everyman Edition, London 1906, pp. 354-5.

book to rejoice or console us; the springs of freshness and feeling are
not there to create such personages. Emma Bovary follows a course in
some respects like that of Anna, but where, in Emma Bovary, is Anna's
charm? The treasures of compassion, tenderness, insight, which alone,
amid such guilt and misery, can enable charm to exist and to emerge,
are wanting to Flaubert. He is cruel, with the cruelty of petrified
feeling, to his poor heroine; he pursues her without pity or pause, as
with malignity; he is harder upon her himself than any reader even, I
think, will be inclined to be.[9]

The contrast here suggested by Matthew Arnold has been
taken up and deepened by many later critics — by none more
tellingly than J.P. Stern, who adds to the discussion another
novel whose theme is also adultery: Theodor Fontane's *Effi
Briest*. In a series of detailed analyses Stern demonstrates that

Flaubert's preoccupation in *Madame Bovary* is predominantly psychological, and the consistent judgement he passes on his heroine is
fastidious or 'aesthetic'. Fontane's preoccupation in *Effi Briest* is social:
in that sphere he passes no direct judgements: but he implies an
outlook of tolerant humaneness which is embodied in one or two
characters on the margins of society, but which is alien to that society
and to the code by which it lives. The line of Tolstoy's narrative in
Anna Karenina is moral, and he shows the moral law at work in a
passionate character, that is, in the kind of character that can most
fully and most consistently exhibit morality in a novel.[10]

And again, after a close consideration of the three heroines'
relation to their children:

To Anna all the world appears as one monstrous accusation, one great
cry for punishment. Morality is for her neither gently implied (as it is in
the ironical tolerance of Fontane), nor is it deflected beyond her range
of awareness (as Flaubert deflects it beyond Emma's range). It is here
fully expressed and fully sustained. Tolstoy evokes it as inexorably as
Dante had invoked Christian morality in the punishment of Paolo and
Francesca; but again, as in Dante, the full meaning of the punishment is
inseparable from the beauty of the trespass, from the splendour of
Anna's pride. In the bodying-forth of this conflict lies the true aesthetic
of the great work of art.[11]

[9] Matthew Arnold, *Essays in Criticism*, Second Series; essay on 'Count Leo
Tolstoy', first published in 1887.

[10] J.P. Stern, *Re-Interpretations: Studies in Nineteenth-Century German Literature*, London 1964, pp. 335-6.

[11] ibid., p. 339.

That places the three novels firmly within the context of their authors' differing methods and achievements, makes sure we do not condemn a herring because it is not whipped cream — but the accent on taste, the valuation, is nevertheless there. Once again it is *Anna Karenina* which emerges as the greatest and deepest work, the work in which our moral as well as our aesthetic nature can feel itself most fully engaged and satisfied.

A good deal of effort in comparative literary studies and observations has, in fact, rightly gone into preventing the wrong value-judgements: into distinguishing different modes and styles each of which has its own justification. In the era of the 'New Criticism' it was particularly important to establish that the methods of minute stylistic exegesis, the methods so brilliantly used by Auerbach, were not equally appropriate to every author. Lionel Elvin, for one, provided a salutary corrective:

This [. . .] kind of exercise [. . .] may tempt the student to over-praise those poets whose powers in the use of language are best revealed in the study of short passages, and to underestimate those who lend themselves to this test less. Keats is bound to come out of it better than Shelley, Pope will come out of it better than Byron, Donne will come out of it better than Chaucer;[12]

while Philip Rahv, in a comparison of Dostoevsky and Proust, attempted an international typology of styles which is well calculated to counteract the temptation Elvin had noted:

Dostoevsky's style has a kind of headlong, run-on-quality which suits perfectly the speed of narration and the dramatic impetuosity of the action. But in itself, if we set out to examine it in small units, it is not rewarding. The principle of Dostoevsky's language is velocity; once it has yielded him that, it has yielded nearly everything that his dramatic structure requires of it. The exact opposite of Dostoevsky is a novelist like Proust, whose themes and structures are undramatic [. . .] The intrinsic nature of Proust's themes and his conception of them as 'enchanted realms', as he put it, in which 'the dust of reality is mixed with magic sand', are such that they demand a master of language for their realization. It is pointless, however, to ask of a novelist whose themes do not require such an intensive stylistic effort that he

---

[12] Lionel Elvin, *Introduction to the Study of Literature*, I, ed. cit., p. 10.

captivates us through language when he is quite capable of captivating us through other means.[13]

This formulation is not entirely happy — in the end every writer can only 'capture us through language', for he cannot reach us in any other way; but the general point made in this passage is surely sound.

Rahv, it is worth noting, is not led to abandon value-judgments in his effort to distinguish between different types of style and the critical approaches they demand; elsewhere in the same collection of essays he has a piece on Gogol and Melville which endeavours to do justice to the former's *Overcoat* and the latter's *Bartleby* without concealing the grounds on which, in the end, the first is preferred to the second: 'Melville's story [. . .] lacks the inner coherence, the resonance and marvellous stylization of Gogol's master-piece.'[14] In the same way Albert Cook, in *The Meaning of Fiction*, after distinguishing various ways of combining evocations of the real world with symbolism (in Jane Austen, Flaubert, Chekhov and D.H. Lawrence) ventures an unfashionable criticism of Lawrence: Lawrence's 'symbolic animals, the horse in *St. Mawr*, the fox in *The Fox*, seem illegitimately to transcend the meaning given them in the novels. They are observed. And they are metaphorical. But their metaphor is at once too symbolic and not symbolic enough. They have neither the one-for-one correspondence of Flaubert's analysis nor the breath-taking concreteness of detail in Turgenev and Chekhov. They are meant to bear a weight of meaning, a message which the form of the story cannot sufficiently contain [. . .] There is a gap between St. Mawr the real horse and St. Mawr the symbol of glowing bodily assertion. Flaubert's *fiacre* has no gap: its rattling, its blackness, its blinds symbolize, and *are*, the disequilibrium, the moral vacancy, the deliberate exclusions, of Emma [Bovary]'.[15] Here Cook's adverse criticism derives its strength from wide-ranging comparisons which refer back to

[13] Philip Rahv, *Literature and the Sixth Sense*, Boston 1969, pp. 240-1.

[14] ibid., p. 200.

[15] Albert Cook, *The Meaning of Fiction*, ed. cit., pp. 173-4.

earlier, more detailed analyses. They enable him to 'place'
D.H. Lawrence's work in an international as well as an
English context.

Some of the most valuable comparisons of this kind
juxtapose two contemporary or near-contemporary writers,
working in different countries, in order to sharpen awareness
of the different forms, which one and the same literary or
cultural movement could take in the countries concerned.
Graham Hough's *The Last Romantics* traces many links
between French Symbolism and the English aesthetic movement of the 1890s and then goes on to contrast two central
figures: Baudelaire and Swinburne. Swinburne, Hough tells
us,

is read [. . .] as a virtuoso on the English metrical keyboard, much of
whose significance lies in his versification for its own sake. The dash
and vitality of his best verse is at the service of a rather monotonous
range of ideas, and his best effects are as a rule merely verbal. To say
this is not merely to depreciate his work; poetry is made with words;
but it is to warn us against looking in him for kinds of significance that
are not there [. . .] The habit of dwelling on the perverse and the
horrifying which [Swinburne and Baudelaire] have in common is quite
differently motivated in the two men. In Baudelaire it is not the result,
or merely the result, of *mésaventures biographiques*, it is the expression
of metaphysical disgust, the final horror of a man who believes in
original sin, but not in the existence of God. Swinburne in comparison
with him remains a naively rebellious asserter of romantic liberty, with
specialised sexual tastes [. . .] [Baudelaire's] perversities and disgusts
are not the eccentricities of a temperament, but powerful symbols of
something that is omnipresent in human life — what Baudelaire himself,
however untheologically, called original sin [. . .] So, at the end of the
introduction to *Les Fleurs du Mal*, 'hypocrite lecteur, mon semblable,
mon frère', cannot but be acknowledged by anyone who has really
discovered what Baudelaire was writing about. I doubt if Swinburne, or
any of the later writers, Wilde or Dowson, who drew directly or
indirectly from Baudelaire, ever began to realise this.[16] They dwelt
rather on the difference between themselves and their fellows: with the
result that their eccentricities remain eccentricities, their confessions
remain at the best private documents; at the worst, that most disgusting
of all kinds of literature, the intimate confession paraded before the
public in fancy dress. Baudelaire became the starting-point for a whole

---

[16] I would disagree with Hough here: Wilde did realize this by the time he came
to write *The Ballad of Reading Gaol*, but he was unable to give it valid poetic
expression.

new generation of writers; in France we have the symbolists, one of the greatest and most far-reaching of modern literary schools; in England we have only the nineties.[17]

As Baudelaire is here used to 'place' Swinburne, so Huysmans and Gautier are used to 'place' Wilde — and through him a whole generation of writers attempting, in France and in England, to find some sort of accommodation between art and a bourgeois industrial society. But the weaknesses revealed, through such juxtapositions, in Swinburne, Wilde, George Moore and the poets of the Rhymers' Club, themselves throw into relief the achievements of the one major figure that emerged from their midst: W.B. Yeats.

They represent a phase through which the poetic sensibility had to pass before it could emerge into new territory. But the taking of a new step in poetry is a more arduous process than the Rhymers supposed, or were capable of. Of their circle Yeats alone had the tenacity and spiritual energy to carry it through. And in considering him we shall have to consider the fusion of this French and English aestheticism with an Irish element that was permanently to change and enrich it.[18]

The study of influence and assimilation across national and linguistic boundaries, the study of tradition and innovation in a wider European as well as a more narrowly British context, and mutual 'placing' through comparison and contrast, all play their part in Hough's stimulating study.

One other type of comparative analysis must not go unmentioned: that which seeks to describe different works of world-literature as the product, and as the revelation, of different personality-types. A distinguished example of this approach may be found in Leon Edel's *The Psychological Novel, 1900-1950*. Here, as a characteristic instance, is Edel's comparison of Proust and Joyce:

In the case of Proust, continual illness had fostered the living and reliving of his novel within the tight walls of his cork-lined room [. . .] — almost as if the room itself had become his mind in which thoughts could flow, unmolested by the ruder temperatures and sharper lights of the world outside. As in psycho-analysis the patient is isolated

---

[17] Graham Hough, *The Last Romantics*, London 1949, reissued 1961; pp. 192-4.

[18] ibid., p. 215.

from external stimuli that his mind may play over the past and link it to the present, so Proust in his soundproofed isolation could practice his extraordinary self-analysis. The present assailed him too violently; immediate experience erupted into allergies and the ills of the flesh. In the past there was tranquillity — and discovery. By the process of remembering, he found himself.

Experience for Joyce took quite another form. Near-blind from his childhood, he lived in a world of sound, in the ceaseless clamour of the city of his youth, Dublin, which he carried with him whether he was in Trieste, in Zürich or in Paris — and in the end all the cities blended in an ever-increasing din, and their languages mingled, so that Joyce's mind became a tower of Babel. Unlike Proust, However, Joyce wanted to catch the present, the immediate moment of perception — he called it an 'epiphany', applying the religious word to his artist's vision. For Proust Time Past could become Time Present, to fade immediately into Past again; for Joyce Time Present was all-important — a continuum of Present, in which the Past inevitably lingered.[19]

A gifted biographer has here illuminated two of the major styles of twentieth century literature through comparison and juxtaposition of life-styles as well as literary modes and techniques. The broad contrast drawn by Edel is not made less illuminating by our awareness that aural impression play an important part in *A la recherche du temps perdu,* and that visual, imagistic elements are powerfully present in *Ulysses.*

A more historically orientated confrontation has been attempted by Lionel Trilling in his essay 'The Fate of Pleasure: Wordsworth to Dostoevsky'.[20] Here Dostoevsky's *Notes from Underground* are examined in a double context: that of Russian and European meliorism and optimism (which crystallized, for Dostoevsky, in Chernyshevsky's Utopian novel *What Is To Be Done?*) and that which Trilling calls a 'conscious commitment to pleasure' in European literature of the eighteenth and nineteenth centuries. In order to sharpen our awareness of the ideas and attitudes adopted and personified by Dostoevsky's anti-hero, Trilling contrasts them with those implied or expressed in the work of many earlier European writers — Wordsworth and Keats among

---

[19] Leon Edel, *The Psychological Novel, 1900-1950*, New York 1955, p. 17.

[20] Lionel Trilling, *Romanticism Reconsidered*, ed. N. Frye, New York 1963.

them. The two English poets, he tells us, are connected by nothing so much as their conscious commitment to the principle of pleasure; but at the same time, Trilling assures us,

> nothing so much separates Keats from his great master as his characteristic way of exemplifying the principle. In the degree that Wordsworth's pleasure is abstract and austere, for Keats it is explicit and voluptuous. No poet ever gave so much credence to the idea of pleasure in the sense of 'indulgence of the appetites, sensual gratification', as Keats did, and the phenomenon that Sombart describes, the complex of pleasure-sensuality-luxury, makes the very fabric of his thought.[21]

In this way Trilling uses two English poets whom Dostoevsky had almost certainly never read to 'place' *Notes from Underground* in the history of European thought and feeling while keeping us aware, also, of the social background of the two poets (the reference to the work of the sociologist Werner Sombart is wholly characteristic), and of the temperamental and ideological differences between them.

Edel and Trilling, sensitive though they both are to literary nuances, lead us nevertheless beyond the frontiers of purely literary analysis; and this, as we have now seen so often, is something that may legitimately happen in most kinds of comparative investigation. There have been attempts at 'placing' works and authors which have led even further from the literary centre without losing their relevance to the literature scrutinized; the analysis, for example, of works by Knut Hamsun which Leo Löwenthal, a sociologist of pronounced literary tastes, attempted in the early thirties of this century.[22] Löwenthal compared the way in which this contemporary Norwegian writer depicted impressive elemental manifestations of nature with that in which these same phenomena are depicted and interpreted in the works of eminent German writers and philosophers of the eighteenth century. Kant, for instance, saw thunderstorms as demonstrations of the sublimity of nature that afforded occasions of showing the even greater sublimity of the human soul; for

[21] Trilling, op. cit., pp. 80-1.
[22] Now conveniently reprinted in Löwenthal's *Literature, Popular Culture and Society*, Englewood Cliffs, New Jersey, 1961.

Hamsun, on the contrary, such storms demonstrated rather the littleness and insignificance of the individual human being. From a series of such observations Löwenthal constructed an image of the social attitudes implicit and explicit in Hamsun's work which led him, correctly as it turned out, to diagnose Hamsun's sympathy with fascism.

Sociological 'placing' is only in its infancy in comparative literature, despite the pioneering efforts of Georg Lukács, the more recent work of Lucien Goldmann, and that of teams of researchers, led respectively by Richard Hoggart and Roger Escarpit, at the Universities of Birmingham and Bordeaux. Such placing can make use of a multitude of separate, often humble observations like those of W.H. Bruford, for instance, who calculated the income of eighteenth-century German and English writers and concluded that Sir Walter Scott earned more from literature in three years than Goethe in all his long life;[23] the table in which Roger Escarpit juxtaposes the social origins and professions of French and German writers in the nineteenth century;[24] or George Steiner's correction of a remark by Lionel Trilling:

Lionel Trilling remarks that 'every situation in Dostoevsky, no matter how spiritual, starts with a point of social pride and a certain number of roubles'. This is misleading so far as it suggests that determining core of economics and stable social relations which we find, notably, in the novels of Balzac. Raskolnikov desperately needs a certain number of roubles, as does Dimitri Karamazov; and it is perfectly true that Rogojin's fortune plays a vital role in *The Idiot*. But the money involved is never earned in any clearly definable manner; it does not entail the attenuating routine of a profession or the disciplines of usury upon which Balzac's financiers expend their powers. Dostoevsky's characters — even the neediest of them — always have leisure for chaos or an unpremeditated total involvement. They are available day and night; no one need go and ferret them out of a factory or an established business. Above all, their use of money is strangely symbolic and oblique — like that of kings. They burn it or wear it over their hearts.[25]

---

[23] cf. W.H. Bruford, *Germany in the Eighteenth Century: The Social Background of the Literary Revival*, Cambridge 1935; new (paperback) edition 1965, p. 279.

[24] cf. R. Escarpit, *Sociologie de la littérature*, 4th edition, Paris 1968, pp. 44-5.

[25] George Steiner, *Tolstoy or Dostoevsky*, Harmondsworth 1967, pp. 142-3., cf. Donald Fanger's contrast, implied in his allusion to *Great Expectations* and *Illusions perdues*, between Dostoevsky, Dickens and Balzac: '[Dostoevsky's]

Such observations are valuable means to a clearer view not only of different artistic personalities but also of the different societies in which they worked, by which they were shaped, and whose self-image they, in turn, helped to modify. The relationship of literature to society is a problem whose complexity continues to fascinate comparatists along with other scholars and critics; many views are possible, justifying, at different times and from a different perspective, such terms as 'reflection', 'determination', correspondence', 'homology', 'affinity', 'expression', 'symbolization', 'rejection' or 'revolt'. One rule holds good, however, in all attempts to relate literature to social or political facts — a rule enunciated many years ago by Ernst Kohn-Bramstedt and given wide currency by Wellek and Warren: 'Only a person who has a knowledge of the structure of society from other sources than purely literary ones is able to find out if, and how far, certain social types and their behaviour are reproduced in the novel. . . . What is pure fancy, what realistic observation, and what only an expression of the desires of the author must be separated in each case in a subtle manner.'[26] What is here said of the novel applies, *mutatis mutandis,* to other literary form and genres.

Some of the subtlest sociological 'placing' of writers and works of literature has come, not surprisingly, from critics working in France. Robert Minder's *Kultur und Literatur in Deutschland und Frankreich*[27] enshrines a multitude of valuable observations about the differing relationship between artists and society in two European countries. Taking off from a consideration of school primers and popular anthologies, its opening essay illustrates, with a wide range of telling examples, the greater alienation of the German writer from the society in which he lived and to which, in the first instance, he had to speak. To bring this difference home

---

heroes are not only outside the dominant classes; they despise them. Their great expectations, their lost illusions, are not social.' *Dostoevsky and Romantic Realism*, ed. cit., p. 134.

[26] Wellek and Warren, *Theory of Literature*, ed. cit., p. 104.

[27] Robert Minder, *Kultur und Literatur in Deutschland und Frankreich*, Frankfurt 1962.

Minder uses what can only be called 'super-imposition' devices:

> It is a tragic paradox that the greatest Prussian king, Frederick II, should be among those most directly responsible for the failure to integrate German poets into society [. . .] Potsdam could and should have become the German counterpart of Versailles. Imagine what a catastrophe it would have been for French literature if Louis XIV had rejected Racine, La Fontaine, Boileau and Molière, had surrounded himself only with Spanish poets, had recognised only Spanish as the language of civilised people![28]

The opportunities Frederick the Great missed by his encouragement of minor French writers, and by his rejection of Lessing, Goethe, Herder and Wieland, could not be more forcibly brought home that in this contrast between his attitudes and those of Louis XIV. Minder does not minimize, however, in his analysis of the consequences that flowed from this and similar rejections, the special insights that German men of letters have derived from their less favourable and less central social position, and values their very different achievement as highly as that of French authors. He uses sociological and historical data freely to illuminate the course of two literatures and to 'place' the achievement of many writers. He recognizes at the same time — and this helps to make his analyses exemplary — that a 'better' social system need not imply a 'better' literature; that art, while bearing (as all human creation must) the marks of its age, may yet transcend the historical limitations to which its creators are subject.

[28] op. cit., p. 15.

10.
Theory and Criticism

When looking, in Chapter 8, at Wellek's distinction between different meanings of the word 'Symbolism', we already skirted what Harry Levin called 'critical lexicography': 'the method of defining key-terms by analysing what they have signified to those who shaped their significance'.[1] Wellek has tackled such terms as 'Baroque', 'Romanticism' and 'Realism' on comparative lines;[2] Levin has examined 'Realism', 'Classical', 'Tradition' and 'Convention';[3] and an International Dictionary of Literary Terms has been in preparation for many years under the auspices of the International Comparative Literature Association. Such critical lexicography involves comparisons at all stages and all levels, as scholars try to trace the changes of meaning that a term underwent in its travels from one country, one social setting, one language to another. It will investigate, for instance, what happened to Plotinus's *endon eidos* when it became Shaftesbury's 'inward form' and Goethe's 'innere Form';[4] or trace the progress of the term *avantgarde* from a military to a political to a literary metaphor; or seek to find out what happened to Aristotle's terms *katharsis* and *phobos* in Dacier and Corneille, in Gottsched and Lessing:

Catharsis [. . .] in the Aristotelian construction [. . .] referred in a very practical, downright and medical way to a supposed capacity of tragic

---

[1] Harry Levin, *Refractions: Essays in Comparative Literature*, Oxford University Press 1966, p. 32.

[2] René Wellek, *Concepts of Criticism*, Yale University Press 1963.

[3] Harry Levin, *Contexts of Criticism*, Harvard University Press 1957, and *Refractions*, loc. cit.

[4] See Chapter II of Peter Salm's *Three Modes of Criticism*, Cleveland 1968.

drama to cleanse our minds of painful and unhealthy emotions. Yet through religious and lustratory metaphoric interpretation the notion was susceptible of being sublimed [*sic*] to mean something like a purifying and exalting of the emotions themselves. This interpretation seems to have appeared even during later antiquity, in neo-Platonic thought. But its hyper-development, to the eclipse of purgative Aristotelianism, was a modern accomplishment. The first step in a fairly plausible evolution was to say — as we may notice, for instance, the Dutch critic Daniel Heinsius saying, and later Milton — that purging the emotions meant tempering or moderating them, to a just proportion in our temperamental equilibrium.[5]

Such studies merge into those of translation and *trahison créatrice*: we can be sure, for instance, that whatever Aristotle meant by *phobos* it was not 'pity turned back upon ourselves', *das auf uns selbst bezogene Mitleid* in Lessing's sense; yet in the history of the drama such misinterpretations had significant causes and important results which make them more than historical curiosities and justify a comparative scrutiny. In the same way, it is worth while studying the reception and application of critical maxims: the history of the different interpretations, attacks and defences to which Horace's maxim *ut pictura poesis*, for instance, has been subjected, is likely to throw a good deal of light on the practice, as well as the theory, of European literature from Roman times to the end of the eighteenth century.

A sketch of different reactions to Horace's maxim involves the confrontation of different theories of literature. Such confrontations are becoming more and more frequent, and may take many forms. In Northrop Frye's *Anatomy of Criticism*, for instance, we find an explicit contrast between 'the aesthetic and the creative, the Aristotelian and the Longinian, the view of literature as product and the view of literature as process';[6] and few historians of criticism can avoid facing the conflict between a critic like Brunetière, for whom the question of genre is central, and Benedetto Croce, who would see every successful work as literally *sui generis*. Often such contrasts serve merely as a prelude to synthesis. H.R. Jauss's confrontation of Formalist and Marxist

---

[5] W.K. Wimsatt and C. Brooks, *Literary Criticism: A Short History*, London 1957, p. 291.

[6] Frye, ed. cit., p. 66.

approaches[7] serves principally to introduce his own 'aesthetic
of reception': a critical method which takes account of the
range of expectation characteristic of a given public and the
way in which authors fulfilled, or disappointed, or influenced
and modified, such expectations.

Comparative criticism has its source-study too. An excellent example will be found in Geoffrey Shepherd's Introduction to his edition of Sidney's *An Apology for Poetry*
(London 1965), where Sidney's originality appears the
brighter because of what we can see him take from many
sources. We learn to appreciate the Horatian, the Ciceronian
and the Platonic strain in European criticism and watch
Sidney reinforce this by 'a firmer if still indirect knowledge
of Aristotle than had been possessed by any earlier theorizer
on poetry in England';[8] we see him make other combinations
and selections, and graft what he learnt abroad on English
habits and on English education. Much that a modern reader
would miss, or misunderstand, becomes clear once we
recognize the European sources and parallels Geoffrey
Shepherd adduces; and Sidney's stylistic distinction becomes
even more obvious once we realize how *An Apology for
Poetry* adopts and varies a traditional form, the 'oration
laudatory of art', with its traditional sub-divisions and
rhetorical devices.

In comparative criticism, as in other comparative literary
studies, it is possible to compile useful histories of fortune
and reputation. There is much point, for instance, in studying
the change of allegiance, in eighteenth-century Germany,
from French to English theories — or rather the way in which
what German writers learnt from the theorists of French
classicism and the French Enlightenment was supplemented,
and modified, by what they learnt from Shaftesbury, Young
and Robert Wood. There is much point, too, in attempts to
pinpoint one fateful encounter in the history of criticism —
that pivotal moment, for instance, in which Dryden encountered the *examens* of Corneille:

---

[7] Notably in *Literaturgeschichte als Provokation der Literaturwissenschaft*
Konstanz 1967.

[8] Geoffrey Shepherd (ed.), *An Apology for Poetry* by Sir Philip Sidney, London
1965, p. 45.

Dryden owes Corneille a double debt as a critic: first he borrows heavily from Corneille's theoretical views, especially from his liberal view of the three unities in the third *Discourse*: and second, he takes confidence from Corneille's *examens* to embark on a pioneer attempt at literary analysis of an English poem. There was simply no English source from which he could borrow an example of critical analysis.[9]

It is meaningful also to compare the thoughts of different theorists, at different times and in different countries or societies, about central questions involving both theory and critical practice; to trace, for instance, with Werner Krauss,[10] the concept of 'levels of style', and its correspondence to social levels, from Donatus and Johannes de Garlandia to Santillana and Scaliger. It is meaningful, finally, to demonstrate how a long-established, coherently developing critical theory may be stood on its head: as when Wimsatt and Brooks show Peacock's attack on poetry in *The Four Ages of Poetry* to be part of the same European development which also produced Shelley's *Defense*:

Except for the transvaluation, the accent of rejoicing rather than lament as science is supposed to deprive poetry of its dominion, [Peacock's] evolutionary account of poetic and cultural origins is the same as that which appears in Vico, in the Germans from Herder on, in Rousseau, and in 18th-century British primitivists like Monboddo and John Brown. And substantially the same account appears in the excited retort which Peacock elicited from Shelley.[11]

The connection between attacks on, and defences of, poetry, from Plato to Tolstoy, is an interesting aspect of comparative literary history that has yet to find its chronicler.

The questions so far raised are all faced, at various points, in René Wellek's *History of Modern Criticism* 1750-1950, of which four volumes have so far appeared. Wellek keeps constantly in mind certain 'key-concepts' (corresponding to Lovejoy's 'unit ideas') while concentrating, rightly, on the exposition of individual systems and individual critics. He seeks to demonstrate 'the individuality and personality, the

[9] George Watson, *The Literary Critics,* Harmondsworth 1962, p. 44.

[10] Werner Krauss, *Grundprobleme der Literaturwissenschaft,* Hamburg 1968, p. 56 ff.

[11] Wimsatt and Brooks, *Literary Criticism: A Short History*, ed. cit., p. 417.

peculiar attitude and sensibility' of the major European critics; he tries to promote a 'synoptic understanding of [the] sometimes loosely put together and contradictory systems of individual theorists';[12] and he attempts, at the same time, through juxtaposition and comparison, to establish a hierarchy of importance. Occasionally one feels that his clear view of the origins and diffusion of critical and theoretical ideas blinds him to individual modifications and achievements; that his learned comparison of Coleridge, for instance, with German predecessors and contemporaries like Kant, Schiller, Schelling, the Schlegels and Jean Paul made him miss something of the force and individuality of Coleridge, and led him to undervalue the work of a critic who has proved more capable than any other of 'providing profitable points of departure for twentieth-century critics'.[13] In the end, however, Wellek's synoptic enterprise justifies itself: through its lucid exposition of the views expressed or implied by many different critics; through its clear tracing of many lines of development; through its constant demonstration that the theory of literature, like the history of genres, can be adequately discussed only if one looks beyond the confines of a single national literature; and through its memorable confrontation of different ways of approaching literature and different interpretations of its nature and function:

In Mallarmé poetry absorbs all reality and becomes the only reality; in Zola and Tolstoy and many others art is identified with life and becomes superfluous and finally useless.[14]

On this great and abiding contrast the fourth volume of Wellek's *History* ends. It provides a fitting theme for the consideration of twentieth-century criticism in the eagerly awaited final volume.

[12] Wellek, op. cit., vol. I, p. 11.

[13] George Watson, *The Literary Critics*, ed. cit., p. 130. Wellek is right when he stresses that Coleridge borrowed a great deal without acknowledgement — studies by Norman Fruman, Elizabeth Schneider and others support and strengthen his demonstration. This only increases, however, our sense of Coleridge's importance as a mediator and synthesiser.

[14] Wellek, op. cit., vol. IV, p. 463.

Wellek's *History*, although it does not neglect contrasting or parallel phenomena in one and the same period, is planned as a primarily diachronic account of developments in Europe and America over two hundred years. Its necessary complement is another classic of comparative literary theory and criticism, Renato Poggioli's *The Theory of the Avant-Garde*.[15] Poggioli here gives us a predominantly synchronic view of the strands that go to make up literary Modernism in Europe, isolating four aspects, or postures, or 'moments': 'activism'; 'antagonism'; 'nihilism'; and, lastly, 'agonism', defined as a kind of voluntary self-sacrifice, a movement's willingness to accept its own end as a preparation for the success of future movements. In the course of Poggioli's patient unravelling, other strands are constantly laid bare: different kinds of alienation, for instance (that of the Dandy, that of the Bohemian, criminal revolt, ivory towers, ghettoes); or the co-presence and opposition of 'dream poetics' and 'abstractionism'. Each of these has its history, which Poggioli traces; but it is only together that they make up the complex web of 'avantgarde' art between Futurism and Surrealism.

Between them Wellek and Poggioli raise most of the problems of comparative literary theory and criticism and indicate further tasks. Among such tasks we may include the construction of critical typologies, of which there have been many in recent times. One need think only of M.H. Abrams' distinction between mimetic, pragmatic, expressive and objective theories of literature;[16] or of René Wellek's own division of territory (in *Concepts of Criticism* and *Discriminations*) between sociological, psychoanalytic, linguistic/ stylistic, organistic/formalist, philosophical and 'myth-orientated' critics. Such typologies cut across countries, languages and social systems: but national, ideological and social differences have clearly to be brought out and related where possible. *Geistesgeschichte* in Germany is a different thing from the philosophically orientated criticism of a Santayana or a Lovejoy; Marxist criticism has taken different

[15] Renato Poggioli, *Teoria dell' arte d'avantguardia*, 1962; English edition, translated by G. Fitzgerald, Cambridge, Mass., 1968.

[16] M.H. Abrams, *The Mirror and the Lamp: Romantic Theory and the Critical Tradition*, New York 1953.

directions in the work of Zhirmunsky, Christopher Caudwell, Lukács and Lucien Goldmann; the relation of literary theory to literary criticism is traditionally seen differently in England, in Germany and in France. Even Comparative Literature itself has a history of national division and of evolution along different lines in different countries: M.F. Guyard's *La Littérature comparée* still distinguishes, as late as its 1965 edition, a positivistically orientated 'French' school from an 'American' school that would extend the concept beyond the frontiers fixed by Fernand Baldensperger and Jean-Marie Carré:

> Where there is no 'relation' — of a man to a text, a work to an environment in which it is received, a country to a traveller — the domain of Comparative Literature ends.[17]

Guyard adds that this debate cuts across national frontiers — 'from this point of view there are many 'French' Americans and many 'American' Frenchmen'.

The comparative study of literary theory and criticism pays special attention — like that of literature proper — to the work of mediators: men like Herder, or like T.E. Hulme, whose mediation was across the frontiers of the different arts as well as different countries. The distinctions Hulme drew in his *Speculations*[18] between 'geometrical' and 'vital' art, distinctions — and recommendations — which powerfully influenced Eliot, Pound and Wyndham Lewis and helped to change the course of modern English literature, may be shown to derive in large measure from the work of a German historian of the visual arts, Wilhelm Worringer. It will study the 'blind spots' of such mediators as carefully as their insights: try to fathom, for instance, the reasons why August Wilhelm Schlegel, whose services to the reception of English, Spanish and Indian literature in Germany were unparalleled, should have been so blind to the greatness of classical French drama — reasons which may be sought in the history of German literature (the struggles of Lessing, and Herder, against French cultural hegemony), that of the Romantic

[17] M.F. Guyard, *La Littérature comparée*, Paris 1965, p. 7.
[18] Hulme, *Speculations*, ed. Herbert Read, London 1924.

movement in Germany, and — of course — the political and social history of Europe since the French Revolution of 1789. It will try to see what sides of the work of a great theorist and critic have been recognized, and developed, by others; what Herder took over from Vico, for instance, and what aspects of Herder's work were then developed in nineteenth- and twentieth-century Europe:

The germ of Taine's and Scherer's aesthetic positivism may be found [in Herder]. He anticipates Taine's guiding principles by seeing nation, race, milieu, time and climate as the determinants of art; but his stress on individuality prevents him from moving consistently in this direction.

Existentialist critics have taken over many of their basic theses from Herder. They have in common the conception of man as determined by history and immersed in time, incapable of any judgment independent of the perspective determined by his personality and situation, engaged in a process of development which never fully realizes his potentialities. Marxist criticism has been able to take over from Herder the demand that literature should satisfy the needs of the people to which it is addressed — especially since he proceeds from the assumption that the people [in its other sense, the 'common people', not 'the nation as a whole'] is the 'largest and most honourable' part of mankind.[19]

The history of aesthetic theory from which this account comes also demonstrates another service that comparatists can render the history of criticism: to restore a sense of proportion, to show the relative importance of a body of work like Herder's, and the unimportance of the squabbles between Gottsched and the Zürich critics Bodmer and Breitinger, in a context that looks beyond Germany to Europe and the world.

Last not least: prolonged concern with comparative literary studies brings in its train an interest in literary universals; an interest in structures and systems characteristic of the literature of many times and many places. It is not surprising, therefore, that comparatists should find themselves — as Claudio Guillén has testified — 'called upon more and more to fulfill the theoretical function without which no body of knowledge can emerge from the accomplishments of

[19] Armand Nivelle, *Les Théories esthétiques en Allemagne de Baumgarten à Kant*, 2nd (German) ed., Berlin 1971, p. 176.

literary criticism'.[20] 'Comparative' and 'General' Literature, as we saw at the outset, ever merge into one another. But just as without theoretical concern an individual piece of criticism or literary research is likely to remain 'a modest contribution to chaos', so theorists must constantly go back to submit themselves to first-hand literary experience:

Each of us has known (and can or should return to) his own formative, unforgettable South Sea island: a particular language, a nation, a moment in history, perhaps even a single play or poem fully and decisively understood. Without the lessons drawn from such 'field-trips', literary theory would be bloodless indeed.[21]

The work of a comparatist like Claudio Guillén shows with what profit a distinguished critic and literary historian may move from concern with one national literature to concern with many and yet return, again and again, to his point of origin and first love (Spanish literature in Guillén's case) for inspiration and refreshment. It shows also, by precept as well as example, how a distinguished comparatist goes from criticism to theory, and from theory to criticism, in continuing and fruitful alternation.

[20] Claudio Guillén, *Literature as System: Essays toward the Theory of Literary History*, Princeton 1971, p. 3.
[21] Guillén, op. cit., p. 4.

Conclusion

Comparative literary studies are indeed a house with many mansions; we have entered most of these in this short survey, though we have not peered into every nook and cranny. We have seen the kinds of connection that such studies seek to make. These resolve themselves, first, into studies of various forms of contact which authors and readers speaking one language may have had with works composed in another: contacts which can be direct (as in Heinrich Mann's life-long love-affair with French literature) or mediated (as in Thomas Mann's approach to the work of James Joyce through reading various critical commentaries but not the works themselves). This led to studies of the actions of 'mediators' and the 'fortunes' of various authors and literary works in countries not their own — fortunes which could be studied in letters, journals, reviews, critical exegeses, and traced in literary works whose authors had felt their impact. Such traces could be distinguished into the 'positive' (borrowing, imitation, adaptation, direct quoting, allusion, impulsion towards new and original creations along similar lines) and the 'negative' (counter-poem, parody, travesty, creation along wholly different lines).

We looked, secondly, at various forms of analogy not presupposing direct contact, but pointing to the possibility that similar literary, social, cultural and psychological dynamics might be at work. Such typologies, which may be further refined, are useful only, however, if we remember that no single factor ever works in isolation, that many of them combine, presuppose each other, in each individual case; and that literary study ultimately concerns itself with wholes that can never be causally 'explained'. What matters.

in the end, is the uniqueness of the individual work of art. However, this uniqueness can be fully appreciated only when we know something of the traditions and conventions that have been accepted or modified; when we are conscious of the earlier works an author has used and wants us to know about (as Brecht wants us to know about Shelley's *Masque of Anarchy*, Joyce about the *Odyssey*); when we have held the work against others in the same genre; when we have, in the fullest sense, compared the work with its models, analogues or opposites and mapped its place in the evolution of forms and the history of ideas.

Among the Greeks, in classical times, all literary studies referred to one body of literature, written in one language; and in our day too the first and the most natural comparisons we will find ourselves impelled to make will be between works in the same language and the same national literary tradition. Yet in this present age it is not long before literary studies of any kind find themselves becoming, inevitably, comparative in a wider sense. The examples used in this book have, in fact, been deliberately selected to show that it is not only self-professed comparatists who have made important contributions to Comparative Literature: many of the illustrations were taken from the works of scholars and critics whose chief preoccupation has been with one language, one national culture, but who have found themselves driven inevitably to widen their scope. One way in which this can happen has been described by a French scholar, Albert Béguin, in the introduction to one of the seminal works of comparative criticism:

My starting-point was the French literature of my time, and I looked for correspondences and affinities in the past of a foreign literature which, by a concurrence of chance events, offered itself to my investigation. Perhaps it is not unnecessary to state explicitly that this is in no way a question of influences. It does not matter at all whether such and such reading in German helped Nerval or André Breton to construct his personal mythology. Since we are not here concerned with literature regarded as pure virtuosity of expression and consequently open to all manner of imitation; since our concern, on the contrary, is with a poetry, romantic or modern, that lays claim to approaching a mode of knowledge and coinciding with the poet's spiritual adventure – 'influence' is of very subordinate importance. At the most it encourages greater boldness in an as yet timid attempt, favours the sprouting of a seed or hastens a flowering; but the seed must be there, and must be able to germinate; and that it will never do, if it is authentic, without taking at once a form that is its own. The affinities that create the great families of the spirit are of much greater importance than the way in which ideas and themes are transmitted. I thought that I recognized more and more clearly, between German Romanticism and the French poetry of our present day, the kind of relationship which is due more to similarities in natural constitution than to actual contacts.[1]

Peut-être n'est-il pas inutile de préciser ici qu'il ne s'agit à aucun degré d'un problème d'influence[2] — this is indeed a useful reminder, from a distinguished French scholar, that comparative literary studies in France were never as exclusively orientated towards the tracing and chronicling of actual 'contacts' between literatures as the usual distinctions between a 'French' and an 'American' school might lead us to suppose.

None of us can fail to be aware of other literatures, other languages, other cultures surrounding, pressing upon, entering, modifying our own. Quotations and allusions, mythological and cross-cultural references clamour to be understood. The literary works we read, or see performed, constitute a *musée imaginaire* to which many people have contributed. Novels from Africa and India widen our conception of the expressiveness of the English language by incorporating modes of story-telling, metaphors and constructions taken over from oral traditions. Modern poets in particular have shown themselves aware of the many, multi-national voices sounding in their ears; for H.M. Enzensberger, poetry has become a museum

which echoes with the ghost-like presence of Catullus; in which one can find images that derive from Indian or Bantu poetry; in which there are reminiscences of Japanese haiku, the choruses of Greek tragedies, the verse of the Vedas or of the Metaphysical Poets, the art of fairy-tales and that of madrigals.[3]

---

[1] *L'Ame romantique et le rêve: Essai sur le Romantisme allemand et la poésie française*, Marseille 1937, pp. xviii-xix.

[2] See the second sentence of the passage just quoted in translation.

[3] H.M. Enzensberger, *Museum der modernen Poesie*, Stuttgart 1964, p. 13.

In this situation the comparatist has a vital task. He can help us to orientate ourselves among these conflicting voices. He can show us the value, the specific contribution of each of the cultures he knows from within. He can explain what seems strange and unfamiliar to us by comparison and contrast with our own traditions. He can watch over the health of literature by studying translations, showing their inadequacies where necessary and suggesting ways of improving them by demonstrating what they have missed. He can follow out allusions, analogies, parallels, historical connections wherever they may lead: and seldom, in the modern world, are they wholly bounded by one language, one set of national frontiers. He can study the role of literature in many different societies. He can trace the movement and transformation of ideas, while also widening the narrow experiences to which our existence in space and time condemns us by opening up, for our emotional and intellectual enrichment, a vast storehouse of imaginative experience. He can increase our knowledge and, at the same time, enlarge our sympathies. He can give us that sense of perspective which will allow us to be justly proud of our own literary and cultural traditions without denigrating or undervaluing those of others. He can show us, concretely, how many variations are possible on common human themes while demonstrating, no less concretely, the give and take of literary interchange across the frontiers of languages, of ideologies, of nations and of continents.

There are, without a doubt, many comparative studies which yield nothing of value — because the subject has been chosen unwisely, because the author lacks literary taste and flair, or historical imagination, or an eye for significant facts. The examples cited in this book should have done something, however, to show that valuable comparative studies can be, have been and are being written. I hope they will also have conveyed some of the reasons for my conviction that in our own day comparatists are more necessary than ever before, and that if comparative literary studies did not already exist, we would have to invent them.

Bibliography

A. Some Useful General Studies

Aldridge, A. Owen (ed.) *Comparative Literature: Matter and Method,* Urbana 1969.

Auerbach, Erich. *Mimesis,* tr. W. Trask, New York 1953. *Scenes from the Drama of European Literature,* New York 1959.

Brandt-Corstius, Jan. *Introduction to the Comparative Study of Literature,* New York 1967.

Bowra, C.M. *The Heritage of Symbolism,* London 1943. *The Creative Experiment,* London 1948. *From Virgil to Milton,* London 1962.

Brower, Reuben A. (ed.) *On Translation,* Cambridge, Mass., 1959 and New York 1966.

Croce, Benedetto. 'La letteratura comparata', in *Problemi di estetica,* Bari 1910.

Curtius, E.R. *European Literature and the Latin Middle Ages,* tr. W. Trask, London 1953.

Demetz, P., Greene, T., and Nelson, L. *The Disciplines of Criticism: Essays in Literary Theory, Interpretation and History* (Festschrift for René Wellek), New Haven 1968.

Durisin, D. *Problémy literárnej komparatistiky,* Bratislava 1967.

Eppelsheimer, H.W. *Europäische Weltliteratur.* Vol. I, *Von Homer bis Montaigne,* Frankfurt am Main 1970.

Etiemble, René. *Comparaison n'est past raison: La Crise de la littérature comparée,* Paris 1963.

Fletcher, John. 'The criticism of comparison: the approach through comparative literature and intellectual history', in *Contemporary Criticism,* Stratford-upon-Avon Studies XII, London 1970.

Frenzel, Elisabeth. *Stoffe der Weltliteratur: Ein Lexikon dichtungsgeschichtlicher Längsschnitte,* rev. ed., Stuttgart 1970.

Friederich, W.P. *The Challenge of Comparative Literature and Other Addresses,* Chapel Hill, 1970.

Furst, Lilian R. *Romanticism in Perspective: A Comparative Study of the Romantic Movements in England, France and Germany,* London 1969.

Gifford, Henry. *Comparative Literature,* London 1969.

Gillies, Alexander. 'Some thoughts on comparative literature', in

Yearbook of Comparative and General Literature 1 (1952).

Guillén, Claudio. *Literature as System: Essays towards the Theory of Literary History*, Princeton 1971.

Guyard, Marius-François. *La Littérature comparée*, Fourth (revised) edition, Paris 1965.

Hassan, I.H. 'The problem of influence in literary history: notes towards a definition', *Journal of Aesthetics and Art Criticism* 14 (1955).

Highet, Gilbert. *The Classical Tradition*, Oxford 1949.

Hauser, Arnold. *The Social History of Art*, 2 vols, London 1951.

Höllerer, Walter. 'Methoden und Probleme der vergleichenden Literaturwissenschaft', *Germanisch-romanische Monatsschrift* 11 (1952).

Hough, Graham. *An Essay on Criticism*, London 1966.

Krauss, Werner. *Probleme der vergleichenden Literaturgeschichte*, Berlin 1965.

James, A. Brett. *The Triple Stream: Four Centuries of English, French and German Literature (1851-1930)*, Cambridge 1953.

Jeune, Simon. *Littérature generale et littérature comparée: Essai d'orientation*, Paris 1968.

Levin, Harry. *Contexts of Criticism*, Cambridge, Mass., 1957.

Refractions: Essays in Comparative Literature, Oxford 1966.

'Comparing the literature', *Yearbook of Comparative and General Literature* 17 (1968)

Lord, Albert B. *The Singer of Tales*, Cambridge, Mass., 1960.

Lovejoy, Arthur O. *The Great Chain of Being: A Study of the History of an Idea*, Cambridge, Mass., 1936.

Essays in the History of Ideas, Baltimore 1948.

Lukács, George. *The Historical Novel*, tr. H. & S. Mitchell, Harmondsworth 1969.

Malone, David H. 'The "comparative" in Comparative Literature', *Yearbook of Comparative and General Literature* 2 (1954).

Moser, Hugo, et al. *Europäische Schlüsselwörter*, Munich 1963.

Peacock, Ronald. *The Art of Drama*, London 1957.

Porta, A. *La letteratura comparata*, Milan 1951.

Pichois, Claude and Rousseau, André-M. *La Littérature comparée*, Paris 1967.

Poggioli, Renato. *The Phoenix and the Spider*, Cambridge, Mass., 1957.

The Spirit and the Letter: Essays in European Literature, Oxford 1966.

Praz, Mario. *The Romantic Agony*, trans. A. Davidson, Oxford 1933.

Preminger, Alex, (ed.) *Encyclopaedia of Poetry and Poetics*, Princeton N.J. 1965.

Remak, Henry H.H. 'Comparative Literature: its definition and function', in Stallknecht, N.P. and Frenz, H. (eds.), *Comparative Literature: Method and Perspective*, Carbondale 1961.

'Comparative Literature at the crossroads: diagnosis, therapy and prognosis', *Yearbook of Comparative and General Literature* 9 (1960).

172   *Comparative Literary Studies*

Spitzer, Leo. *Linguistics and Literary History: Essays in Stylistics*, New Jersey 1948.
Savory, Theodore. *The Art of Translation* (new and enlarged edition), London 1968.
Stallknecht, N.P. and Frenz, H. (eds.) *Comparative Literature: Method and Perspective*, Carbondale 1961.
Strelka, Joseph P. *Vergleichende Literaturkritik: Drei Essays zur Methodologie der Literaturwissenschaft*, Berne 1970.
Strich, Fritz. 'Weltliteratur und vergleichende Literaturgeschichte', in *Philosopie der Literaturwissenschaft*, ed. Emil Ermatinger, Berlin 1930.
Texte, Joseph. 'L'Histoire comparée des littératures', in *Etudes de littérature européenne*, Paris 1898.
Thorlby, Anthony. 'Comparative Literature', in *The Times Literary Supplement*, 25.7.1968, and *Yearbook of Comparative and General Literature* 17 (1968).
Trousson, Raymond. *Un Problème de littérature comparée: les etudes de thèmes.* Essai de methodologie, Paris 1965.
Van Tieghem, Paul. *La Littérature comparée*, Paris 1931, 1946.
'Synthèse en histoire littéraire: Littérature comparée et littérature generale', *Revue de synthèse historique* 31 (1921).
Van Tieghem, Philippe. *Les Influences étrangeres sur la littérature française (1550-1880)*, Paris 1967.
Wais, Kurt. *Forschungsprobleme der vergleichenden Literaturgeschichte*, Tübingen 1951.
Watson, George. *The Study of Literature*, London 1969.
Wehrli, Max. *Allgemeine Literaturwissenschaft*, Bern 1951.
Weisstein, Ulrich. *Einführung in die vergleichende Literaturwissenschaft*, Stuttgart 1968.
Wellek, René. *A History of Modern Criticism, 1750-1950*, New Haven 1955 ff.
Concepts of Criticism, New Haven 1963.
Discriminations, New Haven 1970.
Wellek, René and Warren, Austin. *Theory of Literature*, 3rd ed. Harmondsworth 1963.
Will, J.S. 'Comparative Literature: its meaning and scope', *University of Toronto Quarterly* 8 (1959).
Wilson, Edmund. *Axel's Castle: A Study in the Imaginative Literature of 1870-1930*, New York 1931.
Wimsatt, W.K., and Brooks, C. *Literary Criticism: A Short History*, London and New York 1957.
Zhirmunsky, V.M. 'On the study of Comparative Literature', Oxford Slavonic Papers 13 (1967).
Ziegengeist, G., and Richter, L. (eds.) *Aktuelle Probleme der vergleichenden Literaturforschung*, Berlin 1968.

B.   Journals and Year-Books
Arcadia, Zeitschrift für vergleichende Literaturwissenschaft, ed. Horst

Rüdiger.
Comparative Literature (University of Oregon), ed. C.H. Beall.
Comparative Literature Studies (University of Illinois), ed. A.O. Aldridge.
Revue de littérature comparée, ed. Marcel Bataillon and Basil Munteano.
Rivista di letterature italiane e comparate, ed. C. Pellegrini.
Yearbook of Comparative and General Literature (Indiana University), ed. H. Frenz, H.H. Remak and U. Weisstein.
Yearbook of Comparative Criticism (Pennsylvania State University), ed. J.P. Strelka.

See also the Proceedings of the International Comparative Literature Association (AILC/ICLA), the Congrès National de Littérature Comparé, the Féderation Internationale des Langues et Littératures Modernes (FILLM), and the American Comparative Literature Association (ACLA).

C. Bibliographies

Baldensperger, Fernand and Friederich, Werner P. *Bibliography of Comparative Literature*, Chapel Hill, University of North Carolina Press, 1950. Continued in vols. 1-9 of the *Yearbook of Comparative and General Literature*.
Bataillon, Marcel. 'Pour une Bibliographie internationale de littérature comparée,' *Revue de littérature comparée* 30 (1956)
Yearbook of Comparative and General Literature, ed. H. Frenz, H.H. Remak and U. Weisstein, Indiana University, Bloomington, Indiana (Annual Bibliography).

A particularly full, accurate and well-arranged Bibliography will be found in Weisstein, Ulrich, *Einführung in die vergleichende Literatur-wissenschaft*, Stuttgart 1968, pp. 231-48.

INDEX